M000035488

CROSSING ALL LINES

GENE WARNEKE

COPYRIGHT 2019 GENE WARNEKE
All rights reserved.

No part of this book may be reproduced in any form
by an electronic or mechanical means, including
information storage and retrieval systems, without
permission in writing from the writer, except by a re-
viewer who may quote brief passages in a review.

Cover Illustration Copyright 2019 by Mike Harpin

Published by Kindle Direct Publishing

This book is a work of non-fiction based on the true-life
exploits of a real person. Although the people, events and
actions are faithfully recreated, the names of some of the
characters have changed. Dialogue has been invented to invoke
the essence of what was said between the characters.

DEDICATION

To Bill Schneid, who, as a friend for nearly five decades, trusted me to recreate his stories accurately.

To Mike Steen, a bedrock of support and an angel incarnate for so many.

To my wife, Maria, an ex-police officer, and adjunct professor of law enforcement, who assisted me with the writing process and allowed me to occasionally not cook but never get our to doing the dishes.

To my son, John, whose companionship I seek.

To those who protect us on a daily basis with integrity, honor, and compassion.

"I don't have to draw a line in the sand.
I already have one.
It's thin.
It's blue.
It's the law,
and if you cross it,
I will protect it."

- anonymous

CONTENTS

INTRODUCTION

The short stories of *Crossing All Lines* are embroidered recollections of a remarkable man, William (Bill) Harris Schneid (pronounced *Schneed*). Schneid was born and raised in a middle-class New York-Los Angeles Jewish family of high intellect and success. His parents expected him to follow their example and to ascend to the highest levels possible. For instance, he couldn't just be a renowned lawyer, he was supposed to be a famous U.S. Attorney General.

Feeling oppressed and rebellious, he joined the California National Guard right out of high school. Selected from hundreds of thousands of National Guardsmen, he trained and fought in Southeast Asia during the Vietnam War with the Military Assistance Command, Vietnam – Studies and Observations Group. This was a highly classified, cross-service United States Special Operations Unit that conducted covert unconventional warfare operations during the Vietnam War. He was assigned the rank of Lt. Commander to allow him to operate with fewer restrictions and more authority under challenging situations.

After the war, he continued to operate with the Unit as it evolved in scope and operations in dozens of countries across every continent, except Antarctica. His Unit also trained with the Israeli Mossad, who taught them tricks and techniques to improve their operational capabilities. He was a soldier's soldier and has been highly regarded in intel circles throughout his life.

The ethics and expectations that his parents drilled into him growing up stayed with him throughout his life. They would propel him to be the best of his peers, no matter the situation. If he were given an undercover assignment to bust a single cocaine dealer, he would end up busting a whole network of dozens of dealers and their suppliers. He did that when he was sent undercover into the mountain jungles of South America to inspect cocaine production and distribution networks and to make large buys. He came back with not only on-the-ground intel but with wanted cartel lieutenants.

Many of the stories in *Crossing All Lines* illuminate Schneid's struggle against unethical and discriminatory law enforcement officials. If you were highly intelligent and open-minded, loved to dine on and cook gourmet meals and appreciated the arts in the 1960s, you were a square peg trying to fit into a round hole. You just didn't fit in with the other blue-collar guys wearing blue suits washed in the injustice of their bigotry and intolerance. And if you called out your fellow officers for doing unethical and illegal things and report them, you would definitely suffer their wrath.

He escaped his malaise of being a beat cop by becoming a freelance agent with various federal agencies doing surveillance, interrogations, investigations, interdictions, rescues and other national security tasks. Unfortunately, due to national security concerns, Schneid was not at liberty to discuss many things he did with the author.

Schneid's ability to deceive and outwit his opponents, whether they be friend or foe is legendary. Under duress, few people could think faster, fewer could shoot more quickly with deadly accuracy.

Now in his late seventies, he is still an elite licensed private investigator, At the age of seventy-three, he uncovered the most enormous medical fraud scheme in our nation's history. That and decades of successful investigative work and community outreach have garnered him the coveted California Association of Licensed Investigators' "2019 Investigator of the Year" award.

Although recounting some of his life's episodes to the author was not easy and sometimes painful, it has also been cathartic for him. *Crossing All Lines* gives the world a glimpse of this elusive and adaptive unsung national hero who has arrested over 3,000 criminals during a career that has lasted for six decades.

AS A YOUTH & A SOLDIER

The following two episodes in the life of Bill Schneid illustrate his quick wit and problem-solving abilities under pressure as a soldier and as a youth dealing with his family. The first story shows how he tested those skills during the Vietnam War, where the military trained him to be stealthy, lethal and goal-oriented.

SOMEWHERE IN SOUTHEAST ASIA

"Every war has its martyrs — the unsung heroes who sometimes don't even know the rationale behind the war they are fighting. They fight because they are trained to, kill because they are told to and die because they are destined to."
- Anurag Shourie

Military Assistance Command, Vietnam - Studies and Observations Group

The naked North Vietnamese Army (NVA) Major lay face up, spread-eagled on the ground in his secret compound strewn with dead VC taken out by Schneid's eight man unit during a surprise assault. His hands and feet were lashed to stakes as Lt. Colonel Bill Schneid's Laotian translator, Bao, quickly told the major what Schneid was about to do to him if he didn't tell them what they needed to know. They didn't have much time before the Major's NVA troops arrived. Schneid, with two of his eight-man team, knelt beside the major, flipped open a narrow six-inch box and pulled out a thin glass catheter-like tube.

"Major, I hear you've been a naughty boy. Bao here says you've tortured and killed quite a few of his people for giving aid to the government. The Major started to scream and curse at Schneid and Bao.

A radio call came in from Senior Scout on point along the road to the compound.

"Incoming Charlie column walking doubletime. You've got six minutes, top. Rendezvous at point 6 for extraction."

They weren't getting anywhere with the NVA Major, so Schneid slipped on a pair of gloves, grabbed and stretched the man's dick, then slowly inserted the fragile tube into its helmet hole.

"Look here, Bao. His thing is smaller than my pinky."

The Major stopped cursing, sucked in a lot of air, then started to chatter rapidly. Bao relayed to Schneid what he was saying.

"Chief, dey got RPG-7's and artillery ammo caches over der under dos two huts. He got a log, papers and maps inside da one to da right."

"Captain, get your skinny ass over there to confirm. Retrieve the info and set charges at 6 minutes to blow the dump."

Now it was payback time for Boa's family whom the Major had tortured to death. Schneid slid the tube all the way in with a little push to make the tip disappear. He pulled a 22 from his belt with one bullet in the cylinder and set it next to the Major's hand, just out of reach, but obtainable with a little struggle.

"Bao, tell the Major the gun is for him to put himself out of misery from what I'm about to do, then gag him."

"Yes, Sir."

"Now, Boa, you get the honors. Slap his dick as hard as you can."

Boa whacked the Major's dick and the glass inside fractured

into a thousand pieces. The Major screeched insanely.

Charges were set, and they had the military log in hand. The team slipped out of the compound.

Carefully, they made their way through the jungle to their extraction point. Their 45th MACV-SOG recon mission had met its goal and within the hour, barring any surprises, they would be airlifted back to the relative safety of their division base.

Not fifty feet into the dense jungle undergrowth, they heard a 22 pistol round go off.

THE PRECOCIOUS ONE

"I was twelve, then I was twenty. I was never a teenager."
- Bill Schneid

William Harris Schneid grew up in an unusual household full of relatives. Besides himself and his parents, an aunt and two grandmothers that had grown up in Russia lived with them. Although tiny, his maternal grandmother, Irina, "Little Grandmother," was the household boss.

Schneid, just twelve years old, came home with a package under his arm and plopped it down on the kitchen counter next to his mother.

"What's in the package, Bill?"

"My pet duck."

"What! What happened to your duck?"

"Well, he grew up, so I took him to the kosher butcher to kill and clean him. The duck's ready to be cooked."

"You had your duck killed. Why on earth would you do that to the poor thing?"

"You and Dad wouldn't let me have a dog or cat, just this duck, and I got bored with it. Other than cleaning up its mess and feeding it, what was the point of having it? If we were living on a farm, we'd be doing this all the time."

Realizing the real reason for her son's resentment was from not being able to have a regular pet, she said no more and cooked the duck for dinner.

One summer's day, the fourteen-year-old Schneid laid on his bed "reading" a *Playboy* magazine with the door closed doing what young boys often do when Irina walked in and caught him. She immediately grabbed him by the ear and dragged him into the bathroom where she stuck a bar of soap into his mouth.

"You keep playing with yourself, and you're going to go blind."

"Ok, Grandma, how about if I keep doing it until I only need glasses?"

When Schneid was eighteen, Grandmother Irina needed to be transferred from a board and care facility to Cedars Sinai Hospital in Los Angeles for medical care. Schneid's father was shocked at how much an ambulance would cost to move her. Schneid came up with a plan to save his father money and impress him.

He drove over to his friend's ambulance company in Van Nuys wearing an Army surplus camouflage uniform.

"Carl, would you loan me one of your ambulances for an Army public relations photoshoot? It's for a television commercial."

"Oh sure, no problem at all."

Schneid was running late, and he had to pick up his friend Jim before heading to the board and care. So he put on the lights and siren to clear the way through traffic. Jim was waiting for him in front of a local junior college. Students and teachers stopped to look as Jim jumped in.

"Here's a camou uniform for you."

Off they went, but this time with only the lights on.

They pulled up to the board and care facility, brought out a gurney and went in to pick up Irina. The charge nurse greeted them. "We didn't call an ambulance for Irina today. What's going on?"

"You don't know who she is?"

"Well, of course, we know who she is. She's Irina."

"Right, but do you know what Irina used to do?"

"No, what did she used to do?"

"Well, she was the head stewardess on Air Force One for the President."

"Oh my goodness! I had no idea of her celebrity status. Staff, we need to get Irina prepped and out of here asap!"

With Irina safely secured in the back of the ambulance, Schneid saluted the charge nurse then drove off to Cedars Sinai with the ambulance's flashing lights on and siren blaring.

When his father found out that Irina had been safely transferred in an ambulance, he asked Bill, "Son, how the hell did you get Irina transferred to Cedars in an ambulance for free?"

"Dad, I have friends in high places."

AS AN UNDERCOVER
AGENT AND BEAT COP

After Schneid returned from Vietnam, he attended the Rio Honda Police Academy and was sequestered to be an undercover cop because of his quick wit and military field experience. After five years of undercover work, he became a beat cop for the Los Angeles Police Department. LAPD loaned him to Bell Gardens PD and Pomona PD for regular beat and multi-agency task force assignments.

These were challenging times for Schneid. He worked long exhausting hours, often doing double and triple work shifts to meet his regular and undercover duties. His fellow officers didn't appreciate his open-minded intelligence, so he was considered an odd-duck and suffered the consequences of their bigotries and hypocrisies.

Although police brass refused to recognize many of his courageous achievements, he did not always go unnoticed by the media. He appeared on television or became the focus of television episodes, but his identity was always masked for fear of retaliation from his fellow officers.

"BOMBED" WITH A WALKIE TALKIE

" ...when it snows in your nose, you catch cold in your brain."
- Allen Ginsberg

That night, Federal Task Force Special Agent Schneid had arrested two large cartel drug suppliers on narcotics charges. It was a huge bust but he had to snort a lot of their uncut cocaine to make them think he was a legitimate buyer. He didn't get home until around three in the morning. For the past week, he had been snorting way too much coke. His mind was fried and he was starting to get a little edgy and paranoid.

He sat down on the steps in front of his house trying to settle down his mind. Absentmindedly, he gazed into the shadows of his porch and saw a box. He dragged it to him and opened it up. Inside was a marine walkie-talkie. He stared at it.

"How in the hell did this get here? What the fuck is this? Son-of-a-bitch, it's a bomb and somebody's trying to blow me up. "

So, what does any terrified citizen do when they see a bomb?

He calls 911.

"I think I have a bomb here."

The LAPD response was immediate. Their Bomb Squad and a half dozen units arrived and blocked off the streets with their patrol cars.

The first patrolman on the scene asked, "Is this the bomb? Do you know how it got here?"

"I don't know. I just saw it sitting here."

Two detectives from the Special Enforcement Unit arrived and saw the walkie-talkie. A bomb had been found in another walkie-talkie in the San Fernando Valley just two days before, so, they took this situation seriously thinking there could be a connection.

"Sir, please come with us to the car."

The Bomb Squad put a detonator on his walkie-talkie inside a bomb-proof box and blew it up in his front yard. Schneid was already starting to sober up when the muffled blast went off. He began to realize the craziness of the situation he had created. Now it was close to five o'clock in the morning and people were in their front yards and driveways wondering what the hell was going on.

The detectives asked him, "Why would anybody want to kill you?"

"I don't know."

"Well, do you have any enemies?"

Since he was working as an undercover agent, he had to lie, even to the detectives. "I don't have any enemies."

"What do you mean you have no enemies. Everybody has enemies, some more than others."

"I don't have any enemies who would want to blow me up."

The detectives figured Schneid wasn't telling them everything, which he wasn't, so they progressively got more aggressive with him and started giving him a hard time. Finally, they decided to take him downtown for interrogation. He knew he was in for a rough time, so when their backs were turned he swallowed four or five valiums to get his head straight.

They took him downtown to LAPD police headquarters known as the Glass House.

"Again, why would anybody want to kill you?"

The detectives were convinced that Schneid was a member of organized crime and were tough on him. They had no idea that he was working as a Federal Drug Task Force Special Agent and he couldn't tell them. He had to protect his cover, especially to local police for fear that any of them could be corrupt. After hours of interrogation, he got fed up.

"Okay, I've had enough of you two assholes grilling and insulting me. I've been here over three hours. We're done with this interview."

"Yeah, well we're sick of you too. We'll drive you back home."

"No, you won't. Give me a phone and I'll call the U.S. Marshall's office."

"What? Why are you going to call them?"

"Because I don't want to be in the same car with you two. You guys disgust me."

So, he got hold of the Marshall's office and said, "Hey Joe, it's Bill. Can you come over to the Glass House? There are two asshole detectives here that have been interrogating me for hours and now want to take me home, but I don't want to be near them."

"Let me talk to them."

He passed the phone to one of the detectives and Joe said, "This is Marshall Joe Klaussner at the Federal Building. Why are you detaining and interrogating Bill?"

"Oh, nothing much, just questioning him about a bomb threat at his house."

"He thinks you haven't been treating him with enough respect. I'm sending two Marshalls over to you asap to pick him up and take him home."

Two Marshalls walked into the interrogation room. "Hey, Bill, we're here to take you home. We hear these two gentlemen haven't been very nice to you?"

"Yeah, these two dicks think they're hot shit but neither one of them could find his ass with two hands."

The two detectives shrank back into the corners of the interrogation room. Schneid could see them wondering, "Who the fuck is this guy?" The detectives still had no clue who Schneid was and why two Federal Marshalls were going to chauffeur him back to his house. Schneid loved every second of watching them trying to figure him out.

Another thing drove the detectives crazy. Their crime lab had been able to put back together almost all of the pieces of Schneid's walkie-talkie and found a serial number and make. They called the regional Motorola distributor to find out who bought the walkie-talkie.

"Officer, we sold this to a marine store in Venice. They went to the marine store and the store told them they had sold it to a Bill Schneid.

"What? Schneid bought the walkie-talkie he thought was a bomb. Now we're really confused. Why in the hell did he think it was a bomb when it was just a walkie-talkie he himself bought?" At that point, nothing made sense to them.

One of the detectives came by Schneid's house a couple of weeks later and spoke to his partner, Mike. "Listen, we know he's dirty and we're going to get him."

"Oh? Well, good luck with that."

THE FREE DONUTS GUY VS THE THIN BLUE LINE

"As you ramble on through life, Brother,
Whatever be your goal,
Keep your eye upon the doughnut,
And not upon the hole."
- Margaret Atwood

It was late in the night, and the car ahead of him was weaving all over Holt Avenue. Patrol Officer Schneid put on his patrol car lights and gave a couple of short bursts of his siren. The car pulled over, and the driver rolled down his window. Schneid walked up and immediately recognized him as the owner of a local donut shop that always gave free donuts to the cops at my station. Everybody at the station called him the "Free Donuts Guy." Since it was department policy never to accept gratuities, Schneid had never received any of his free donut offers.

"May I see your license?"

The Free Donuts Guy fumbled severely trying to get his license out of his wallet.

"Here it is Offser Schnide."

"That's Schneid. Have you been drinking alcohol, Sir?"

"Yez, Sur, I may haf had a couple."

"Sir, Please get out of the car."

The Free Donuts Guy failed every sobriety test he tried to

perform. Schneid arrested him and took him back to the station where he also failed a breathalyzer test. He was almost twice the legal limit, so Schneid booked him.

The Field Sergeant had known the Free Donuts Guy for years. After Schneid returned from putting him in the drunk tank for the night, the sergeant said to Schneid, "Do you realize who that person is? I need you to rewrite your report saying that the breathalyzer showed he was under the legal limit. He's a good guy, he gives us all free donuts, and he's pro-cop."

"Sir, I'm not going to falsify my report."

"Well, then you're forcing me to write a counter-report that will say, "I observed this person, and he didn't seem to be intoxicated. So, I re-ran the breathalyzer test, and it turned out to be half of what the legal limit is." Schneid refused to budge, so the sergeant retested the Free Donuts Guy and wrote a false report before driving the Free Donuts Guy over to get his car out of impound.

Next morning, Schneid got a call at home from his Patrol Captain. "What the fuck is going on with you and the Sergeant?"

"What do you mean Captain Wallick?"

"I have two reports in front of me. Which one is correct?"

Schneid gave him his version, but unfortunately, the sergeant was very popular with the other officers at the precinct.

"Get your ass down to the station so we can sort this out face to face."

Back at the station in the Captain's office, the Captain said, "We've got two diametrically opposed reports, and I only want to see one report, the correct one."

The sergeant sat silent, but Schneid spoke up. "Captain, mine is the accurate one. I made a good bust, and I'm sticking to it."

"Sergeant, do wish to counter Patrol Officer Schneid?"

"No, Sir, but he arrested the Free Donuts Guy."

"What's our policy toward gratuities, Sergeant?"

Needless to say, the sergeant got suspended without pay for thirty days.

The first night of the sergeant's suspension, Schneid was alone on patrol when he got a dispatch call, "Public disturbance, gang activity, 2100 block, South Gary. All units respond."

"Unit 381. 10-8, 10-4 en route."

Schneid screeched to a stop in the middle of the broad avenue. Before he got out of the car, he called dispatch, "10-30! I repeat 10-30! Officer needs assistance!

Dispatch responded to his 10-30 by calling all nearby units to respond immediately. Usually, that would trigger a major response from all available nearby units.

Over forty gangbangers were going at it with knives and baseball bats. Schneid stepped out of his cruiser and yelled out, "Break it up! Break it up now!"

Within seconds, he and his car were pelted with rocks and pieces of concrete. Before he could duck back into the car, a gangbanger snuck up behind him and whacked Schneid hard across his back with a two by four. Now on his knees, he reached into the car and grabbed his radio.

"10-30, I repeat 10-30! Officer needs help! Officer down and injured."

Dispatch kept calling for all nearby units to respond.

As he was getting the shit beaten out of him, Schneid listened as one unit after another made single clicks on their radios, a signal that they knew he was in danger, but they weren't going to respond and help. Better to remain silent when refusing to support a fellow officer, especially when he had busted the Free Donuts Guy and had their favorite sergeant suspended. The "Thin Blue Line" of mutual protection had been breached, in effect, by donuts.

Dispatch then reached out to neighboring cities for mutual aid. A K9 unit responded. When it came screeching up, the officer let his dog loose on the gangbangers. It worked. The crowd ran for cover, and the fight was history.

Schneid drove to the back of the station, sat in his patrol car and sobbed. He could have been mortally wounded and couldn't believe that the very cops whose lives he had been sworn to protect, and for whom he was willing to sacrifice his life to protect, were ready to let gangbangers beat the shit out of him because he had busted Free Donut Guy.

When the Captain heard about it, he called Schneid into his office. "You know Schneid, I could move you to a different shift while we investigate this."

"No, Captain. I'll deal with these assholes in my own way by just putting up with it. I'm not going to let them run me out of there."

Internal Affairs investigated the incident, but it was eventually covered up. Turns out, the "brotherhood" would remain on the wrong side of the Thin Blue Line. Schneid started to look elsewhere for a truer brotherhood.

THE DAMN BARTENDER

Patrolman Schneid sat in his apartment on his day off drinking wine and cleaning his gleaming six-shot 357 Colt Python revolver. He had checked the cylinder to make sure it was empty of its armor-piercing bullets, bullets that could go through an engine block. On his television, the conclusion of John Wayne's "The Shootist" was near. Wayne's character, J. B. Books was in a pickle.

He adjusted its sights and peered down the six-inch barrel at the bartender who was sneaking up behind J. B. Books with a shotgun. Schneid shouted out a warning to him and plugged away at the bartender: click... click... BOOM!

The bullet blew the TV to smithereens and went through his apartment wall.

"Fuck! I killed my TV!"

Schneid jumped out of his chair and ran outside into his

apartment complex. When a 357 goes off, it's loud, deafening, and the last thing he wanted was for a neighbor to call the police and report a gunshot there.

A few people had already gathered and asked Schneid, "What the hell happened?"

"That stupid TV of mine blew up."

"Oh my, are you alright?"

"Yes, I can't believe it. I hope it's still under warranty."

He reported to work the next day and checked the dispatch log. The assassination of his TV had not been called in. His quick wit had saved his job, but ironically, not J. B. Book's life.

"God damn that bartender!"

WATTS, SHOOTING
FISH IN A BARREL

"Policemen so cherish their status as keepers of the peace and protectors of the public that they have occasionally been known to beat to death those citizens or groups who question that status."
- David Mamet

A Schneid t-shirt made during the Watts' riots.

It was Friday the 13th on a sweltering 1965 August afternoon in Watts. Several Black men lay dead or dying on the sidewalk in front of the supermarket and adjacent furniture store. A dozen LAPD officers in white helmets were taking small arms fire from the stores. Most of the police were crouched behind cars across the street. Some were next to the stores, or behind mailboxes and light poles. Two National Guardsmen pulled up in a jeep with a 30 caliber machine mounted on the back.

The driver called out, "Need some help?"

Detective Schneid responded, "We're almost out of ammo, and there are close to a hundred assholes ransacking the stores. We could use your firepower. All we've got are 38's and 12 gauges. We have the back covered, but there's a fire on that side, so the looters are coming out the front doors and windows. Unless they're holding food, blast their Black asses."

"Ok, we're in position."

Four looters came out of the front door firing pistols while using a large sofa as cover. Simultaneously, several young men flew out of the windows and ran along the sidewalk.

They opened up: bam-bam-tat-tat-tat-bam-bam-tat-tat-tat-bam-tat-tat-tat-bam. They riddled the sofa and looters to pieces. None of the young men survived the volley of bullets.

"Cease fire!"

For the next two hours, the police and guardsmen picked off a couple dozen more looters. The fire at the back had reached the roofs and spread rapidly throughout the stores. In a panic, people ran out of the stores only to be shot dead. Scores were still in the store when the

roof collapsed upon them. Those who weren't shot were incinerated.

"Bill, how many do you think we got?"

"Looks like around forty dead in front. Carl says they've got a half dozen dead in the back and who knows how many died in the fire."

The sergeant gathered his unit together and thanked the Guardsmen.

"Look, what happened here stays here. We're in a war zone and what we did today was justifiable homicide of felons shooting at us during the act of looting. File no reports about this. If Command doesn't ask, don't tell. Understood?"

All nodded in agreement, and the Guardsmen drove off.

"Schneid, the Station says there will be no more ammo for us until 9 pm."

"No worries. I've got plenty of ammo at my house. Let's get up there and resupply before we get reassigned."

As they got into their black and white Plymouth Savoy squad car, one of the officers remarked, "Man, that was like shooting fish in a barrel at an amusement park from hell."

[Note: According to the Coroner's Office, the official death toll for the six days of the Watts' riot was only 34. No police reports were filed regarding the shootout at these two stores.]

THE UNSUNG HERO

"A hero is an ordinary individual who finds the strength to persevere and endure in spite of overwhelming obstacles."
- Bill Reeve

Charlie slept in a drunken stupor in front of his black and white television. Its rays flickered across the walls of his small apartment. The late-night B-grade movie "Zontar, the Thing from Venus," was playing. Actor John Agar was stabbing a bat-like creature in front of his fireplace when Charlie's lit cigarette tipped out of the ashtray and ignited the papers and Kleenex in his trashcan.

At 3:20 am, Officer Schneid turned the corner and saw thick black smoke rising from the third story of the 1930's wooden rooming house. He pulled up and radioed for assistance and full fire response. He left his patrol car's engine running and ran into the three-story dwelling banging on random doors yelling, "Wake up, get out, fire, fire!" He banged and hollered his way through the second floor and then up to the top level looking for the source of the smoke.

Schneid choked as he made his way down the smoke-filled hallway searching for the source of the smoke. He found a hot door, and not knowing any better, busted it down. When he did, the super-heated blast of smoke enveloped him and knocked him backward into the hallway wall. His face and lungs burned. His eyes got seared, and he could hardly see. His nose ran like an open faucet. He staggered away from the blast and backed down the hallway, hitting the walls on both sides. Hacking and coughing, the lack of oxygen finally brought him to his knees on the hard linoleum floor.

Officer Coon yelled out, "Schneid, hey Schneid, are you there?" Schneid could hear him but not see Coon through the smoke, but he mustered enough strength to call out, "I'm over here! I'm over here." Coon pulled him to his feet, and together, they struggled down the stairs. His face blackened from soot and hair singed from the back-draft blast, Schneid was barely conscious. Coon put Schneid into his patrol car just as the fire engines arrived on the scene. With lights and siren blaring, Coon raced Schneid to the closest emergency room.

There, with an oxygen mask strapped to his face and EKG leads sticking onto his sweating chest, he looked up at one of the nurses and apologized, "Nurse, I smell bad, don't I? I think it's the acrid smoke in my uniform."

"Officer Schneid, you just saved over three hundred people, and you're worried about your smelly uniform? You're a hero to all those people. You'll not only get a new uniform, but I'm sure you'll get a medal from the mayor."

The only cop who got an award was Coon for saving Schneid's life. Schneid, the super-cop, gained no recognition for his bravery from the mayor, nor his chief, because he was seen as the department's square peg in the round hole.

SECOND-DEGREE MURDER OR SELF-DEFENSE?

"In time we hate that which we often fear."
- William Shakespeare

"Officer Schneid, I'm at a loss of what to do about Don Jr. He won't listen to us, and now he won't even take our calls. His mother is despondent."

"Don, he's at my house at the moment. Why don't we go over there and have a heart-to-heart talk with him?"

"Can we, right now?"

"Sure, why not. Follow me in your car."

Half-looped, Don Sr. followed Schneid to his house.

When they got to Schneid's house, the father quickly got out of his car.

"Hold on a second, Don. Let me talk to your son first."

Schneid went into his house and found the son. "Don Jr., your dad wants to talk to you."

While teaching Police Explorers, Schneid had a cadet who played soccer at a nearby Christian high school. He got suspended because before one practice, the soccer coach detected beer on his breath. His parents, especially his father, were strict Christians and were furious with their son. His dad was the general manager of a Chevy agency, and his mother was a physician. His dad threw his son out of his house.

The young man asked Schneid if he could stay with him until he turned eighteen and could get a good job. Since he had already been burned over the Donut Man incident and the single-clicks he got, Schneid knew his fellow officers didn't have his back and that the department had eyes on him for any unusual behavior. Having a young man living in his home would undoubtedly give them more than enough ammunition to question his ethics and undermine his career. To get ahead of that antipersonnel landmine, Bill went straight to the Chief.

"Chief, the boy wants to stay with me until he can figure things out. I checked with his parents, and it's okay with them. However, I want his parents to come down here to sign an agreement that says it's okay with them."

Schneid didn't want anything to go wrong. So, they came down and met with the Chief. He gave his approval, and they signed an agreement to allow the boy to live with Schneid until he was eighteen, which he would be in a couple of months.

A couple of weeks later, his father decided to meet with Schneid at a local bar to discuss his son's suspension and what else he might do to punish him into humbleness. Now, he was outside of Schneid's house, ready to act.

Schneid asked the boy, now eighteen, if he wanted to talk with his dad. "Yeah, sure. Send him in, but I want you to sit with us."

Schneid went back to the parking area.

"Your boy says it's okay only if both of us go in."

"That's good with me. You'll get to see his reaction when I tell him I'm going to take his car away. Right now, he doesn't think I'm much of a man, but I'm going to make sure he knows just what kind of a man I am." He lurched his way to the trunk of his car, where he pulled out a gun.

Schneid, unarmed, yelled out, "Don, don't! Put the gun back in the trunk!"

Don Sr. pointed his gun high above him and shot off a round. Don Jr. heard Schneid yell at his father and now heard the gunshot. He thought his dad shot Schneid. So, he went upstairs and got one of Schneid's guns out of his safe box, went back downstairs and laid in waiting on the floor in the living room with the gun aimed at the front door. When his father burst through the front door, Don Jr. immediately opened fire. The first shot hit his dad in the chest and spun him half around. He then quickly fired three more rounds into his dad's back.

Schneid rushed into the house and went to the father crumpled on the floor.

"I'm dying."

"No, you'll be alright. Just hang on." A minute later, he passed.

In Schneid's book, this was second-degree murder. He thought any typical teenager would have run out the back door, scared. Why would anyone wait for somebody armed to come through the front door? A right-thinking person would get the hell out of there, especially if he were only eighteen. The fact that he was armed and laying in wait for his father to come through the door told Schneid that it was murder.

Eventually, Don Jr. pleaded self-defense and got away with it because his father had a gun in his hand that he had just fired. But Schneid knew better. The kid had a choice.

Of course, there was a big stink afterward in Schneid's department. A fellow officer said, "Schneid, you should've jumped at the father when he had the gun?"

"I was unarmed."

"Don't matter. You should have gone for the gun."

"Really? Tell you what. Let's you and me play out the scenario right here, right now."

Schneid emptied his revolver's cartridge and handed it to the cop. Then he stood the same distance he had been from the father.

"I'll come at you, and you see how many targeted rounds you can get off before I reach you."

Schneid went for the big-mouthed cop, and the cop fired off three 'rounds' before Schneid got to him."

"That's why I didn't go for the gun, you stupid shit. I would be dead or dying on the spot, and the father would have been free to get the kid. For a cop, you're one dumb shit."

THE SINGLE BULLET THEORY

"Things Are Seldom What They Seem"
- W. S. Gilbert

It was a hot summer's day in the valley.

"Units 4 and 17 respond. Code 3. Shots fired at 2255 Belinda Drive."

Officer Robbie Stephenson responded first. "Unit 4 en route. Two minutes out."

Officer Schneid responded, "Unit 17 en route."

As he pulled up to the residence, Officer Stephenson was standing next to his car, interviewing neighbors.

"Yes, Officer. We heard only one shot about ten minutes ago."

Both officers walked up to the front door where Schneid pushed Stephenson to the side.

"Robbie, if someone shoots through the door, you'll be a dead man standing."

Schneid rang the doorbell, rapped hard on the door, then called out, "Police officers! Open the door!"

No response. He tried again. Still no response, so he looked in the front window.

"Robbie, I can see the body of a man on a hallway floor in front of a closed door." "Unit 47. We have a body down inside the residence. Ambulance needed."

While Stephenson stayed near the front door, Schneid walked

around the side of the house. He realized the closed door was to a bathroom.

"Robbie, we need to get that hallway guy out of there. He could still be alive."

"I'm not going in there."

"What do you mean you're not going in there."

"There's no way I'm going in there."

Schneid got up into his face. "Robbie, you're a fucking coward."

Without help, Schneid kicked in the front door and dragged the body out. Sure enough, the guy was still alive but unconscious inches from death. By the time the ambulance arrived, he was dead.

Stephenson looked but saw no weapon inside. However, there was a fresh bullet hole in the bathroom door. He figured the shooter was holed up in the bathroom.

"Unit 3. We need tear gas to extract a suspect."

Sergeant Denbo, who Schneid considered to be a moron, showed up with a case of "triple chaser" tear gas canisters. A triple chaser was designed to fragment into three sections to gas-out a large area. It was never meant for small spaces like this bathroom. No matter, Denbo the Moron threw a triple chaser through the bathroom window and filled it with enough gas to paint the walls and ceiling. They waited, but nobody came out.

After a while, Schneid thought, "Whoever's in there must be dead from that much gas." He went back inside the house and rapped hard on the bathroom door.

"This is the police. Is anyone in there?"

No response. He went back outside.

"Robbie, we need to break down the bathroom door."

"I'm not going in there."

They argued until Schneid said to him, "As I said before, Robbie, you're a fucking coward. To your fellow officers, you're a worthless piece of shit."

Pissed, Schneid went back in, busted down the door, and with a gun in hand, entered the gas-filled bathroom. Schneid could make out a man lying motionless on the floor in a pool of blood dead. He had a massive head wound, and next to him was a large-caliber revolver.

Schneid's uniform was made of wool, not khaki, and he was hot and sweating profusely. The tear gas penetrated and chemically seared his skin mercilessly. Pumped up on adrenalin and ignoring the pain, Schneid yanked the man out of the room with a strength he didn't know he had.

Schneid went back in and retrieved the gun. It had only one empty chamber, and he remembered the neighbors said they had heard just one shot.

"How the hell did two men die from just one bullet?"

He put the pieces together. The man in the hallway was the brother of the guy in the bathroom. The brother in the bathroom was threatening to kill himself while his brother was on the other side of the door pleading with him not to kill himself. When the brother shot himself in the head, the bullet continued through the door and into his brother's head. A single bullet had tragically killed both brothers.

For the police department's brass, this was yet another inconvenient act of bravery or heroism by Schneid. He was not of their ilk and was too good at what he did for their liking. In short, he was so good, he made everyone else in that department look bad. So they mocked him with dribble like, "Hey Super Cop, who are you going to rescue today?"

He got no letter of commendation for his act of bravery, nor did he for several other courageous efforts. However, the local Optimist International chapter found out that Officer Schneid had not been recognized for this and other acts of heroism. Incensed, they created a special award for him. They invited the media and the whole police command to a Law Enforcement Appreciation Day ceremony where they awarded Schneid a plaque commemorating his acts of heroism
and the police brass watched in shame.

THE DEADLY BANK
SHOOTOUT

Enrique pulled his gun from under his shirt as he walked up to Teller Heather behind the bank's counter. "Give me all of your cash, now!" His partner in crime, Carlos held a gun to the bank guard's head and yelled out, "Everyone, get down and stay down or I'll blow your brains out!"

LAPD officer Schneid and his partner, Tim Martin, had just cashed their paychecks and had left the bank only seconds before the robbers walked into it. The two cops stopped at the corner to light cigarettes and chat. They then headed for their patrol car and had walked down the alley behind the bank when they heard a gunshot and yelling behind them. They spun around and saw Enrique and Carlos running towards them down the alley followed by the bank's security guard.

Schneid and Martin yelled, "Police! Stop!"

Instead, Enrique and Carlos opened fire on them. An explosion went off in Enrique's bag and threw off his first shot directed at Schneid. A bullet bounced off the dumpster next to Schneid, and another whizzed past his head. He and Martin had both done time with military special ops units and had been in police shootings before. Without thinking, they drew their weapons and fired back with deadly accuracy. Schneid's first 38 hollow-point bullet hit Enrique squarely in the chest. He pumped five more shots into him, all hitting within a five-inch spread. He quickly popped out his empty cylinder, popped in another and directed his fire toward Carlos who was shooting from behind a dumpster. Martin hit Carlos in the leg and shoulder before putting a round through his neck, killing him.

The two bank robbers were down and dead. The whole episode had taken less than twenty seconds. Neither officer had been hit, and the guard was also unscathed.

The officers cautiously walked up to the robbers to check their vitals. Half of Enrique was covered in red. At first, Schneid thought it was blood, but then he realized that Teller Heather had slipped an exploding die pack on top of the money pile inside the robber's pillowcase. It was on a timer fuse and went off during the firefight. That was the bam he heard the same time Enrique shot at him.

The bank, visibly shaking, came over to the officers and said, "Where the hell did you two learn to shoot? Those guys had no chance against you two."

Schneid looked at Martin and then replied, "Worked at a carnival duck-shooting gallery."

When it was all over and done with, Schneid and Martin drove to a bar and spent the rest of that warm Spring day drinking gin tonics to calm down and reflect on what had just happened to them.

"If we'd stayed in the bank twenty seconds longer, we would have been face-to-face with them surrounded by innocent people."

SAVED BY THE FIRING PIN

"Guns require a finger to pull the trigger." - Texas Governor Rick Perry

It was Schneid's habit to always take a shotgun with him whenever he went to a nighttime burglary call. He knew that at night, it was near impossible to hit anything with his revolver, so he wanted to have as much firepower that was available for cops at the time. Plus, if he was inside a building and he racked a shell into the shotgun, burglars could hear the distinctive sound of the loading "shick-shick" of the gun echo all over the place. Several burglars had surrendered when they heard him load. To him, as a cop, it was an effective deterrent.

After a call was wrapped up, he would always clear the round out of the chamber because he didn't want to have a live round in it go off. He would then secure it in its patrol car mount. At the time, cops mounted their shotguns horizontally atop the front transmission hump for quick access.

One night near the end of watch that had two burglary calls, a weary Schneid pulled his cruiser alongside another cruiser to chit-chat. As he talked to the officer in the other unit, he had his left hand on the steering wheel and his right hand resting around the shotgun's trigger. Absentmindedly, his fidgeting finger accidentally pulled the trigger.

BOOM! A round went through the cruiser's firewall and into the engine compartment.

45

Schneid quickly put his right hand on the steering wheel and said to the other cop, "What the hell just happened!"

"I don't know, it sounded like a shotgun going off."

"Oh my god, my shotgun went off while my hands were on the steering wheel."

"Yeah, I can see them." The other officer was a bit of a half-wit anyway.

Not believing Schneid's story, Captain Parker and the department brass thought, "Ah-hah! We've got him now." They put him on suspension per an investigation. Off the shotgun went to Remington for forensic analysis.

Schneid thought, "That's it. I'm done for."

Two months later, the forensics' report came back from Remington. "We regret to inform you that the accidental discharge of the 12-gauge shotgun that you submitted to us was due to a crystallized firing pin."

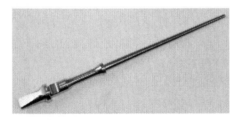

A Remington shotgun firing pin

Captain Parker read the report. "What the hell? I know Schneid pulled that goddamn trigger."

Schneid started believing in God again.

POLICE ACADEMY SHENANIGANS

At the Rio Hondo Police Academy, Schneid taught "Officer Survival and Ethics." The class started at seven in the morning. Attending recruits would come into class after doing strenuous early morning workouts like running up and down hills. Invariably, one or more of them would nod-off in class.

Schneid was getting tired of their inability to focus. So he came up with an idea to keep all of them fully awake. Seeing a few nodders one morning, he stopped his lecture and reached into his briefcase. Out came a CS teargas grenade. With it in hand, he walked up to one of the nodding cadets in the second row.

"Cadet Nadal, you seem to be having trouble staying awake?"

"Yes, Sir."

"Well, then let me help you stay awake to digest the important survival information I'm trying to teach you. Here, take this CS teargas grenade."

He handed the grenade to the cadet.

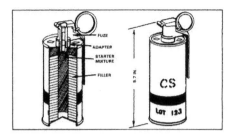

"Cadet Nadal, hold your thumb on the handle and pull the pin out. Don't release your hold on the handle."

With his thumb over the handle, the cadet pulled the pin out as instructed.

"Cadet Nadal, do you know what will happen if you fall asleep and let go of that handle?"

"Yes, Sir, the grenade will go off."

Schneid looked over at Cadet Farnsworth. "Cadet Farnsworth, do you know what will happen if that grenade goes off inside this classroom?"

"Yes, Sir, CS teargas will fill the room, and we will have to evacuate."

Schneid looked at "Cadet Santana, how long does one have before the grenade goes off?"

"Sir, no time, Sir."

Cadet Nadal did not fall asleep that morning. Neither did any of the other cadets. At the end of class, he had Cadet Nadal put the pin back in and give it back to him.

Every morning, Schneid would grab the same CS gas grenade whenever he spotted some cadet nodding off. If the cadet with the grenade started to nod off again, the rest of the class would quickly jostle him or her back awake.

At the end of the last class, Schneid took the grenade out of his briefcase, pulled the pin, and slid it along the floor to the back of the room where it bounced off the wall. The recruits leaped out of their desks and ran for the door, but the grenade didn't go off. It was a dummy grenade that had no gas in it.

The cadets were chagrined and exclaimed, "Oh shit, damn, that's fucked up...," but they also saw the humor in it.

Schneid's tactic had worked. After a few nodding-grenade-in-hand episodes, his class had become perhaps the most attentive in the history of Rio Hondo's Police Academy.

To get certified as an opiate drug expert for court testimonies, LAPD detectives had to take a Drug Recognition Expert class at the Los Angeles Police Academy. Along with another detective, Detective Schneid taught the class. This detective, who was a pay-grade above Schneid, knew that Schneid had used heroin when he had worked undercover.

The detective got a bright idea. "You know, Schneid, it would be very realistic if you shot up some heroin and to let all of the detectives check out how pinpointed your pupils become."

"Are you nuts?"

"Listen, that kind of realism works."

"Are you sure?"

"Yeah. They'll love it."

Schneid saw the perverse humor in crossing another forbidden line, so he said, "Ok. Why not?"

The detective got some heroin out of a closed police case in the evidence locker. Just like it was done on the streets, Schneid cooked up the heroin in a spoon and then sucked it up in a syringe through a small cotton ball. He found a welcoming vein and shot up a small dose, enough to give him just a slight buzz but not enough to impair his judgment.

Sure enough, his pupils became pinpoints. The seasoned detectives were astounded that Schneid would shoot up in front of them. Each one then came up and stared into his eyes, then compared them to the wallet-sized card they carried that gave them the millimeter measurement of pupil constriction so they could include it in their drug bust reports.

The Captain never found out about their performance.

ROBERT KENNEDY & THE WOMAN IN THE POLKA DOT DRESS

"I can understand the Chinese Wall:
it was built as a defense against marauders. But
a wall such as that in Berlin,
built to prevent people from seeking freedom,
is almost beyond comprehension."
- Robert F. Kennedy

At 12:56 am on June 5, 1968, Schneid got a call. "Bill, Earl here. Listen, Kennedy's been shot. He's been shot in the back

three times and once in the head."

"Holy crap. Is he still alive?"

"Barely. He was taken to Good Samaritan Hospital because of the head wound."

"Where did the hit go down?"

"At the Ambassador Hotel in a kitchen pantry adjacent to the Embassy Room where he spoke."

"What was he doing in the pantry?"

"Don't know other than he was re-routed at the last second from the planned exit route, probably because of the large crowd inside the ballroom. I was outside the hotel lobby when I got word of it. I ran into the lobby and an elderly couple stopped and told me that they saw a young couple in their early twenties walking fast down the stairs from the Embassy Ballroom. The couple was smiling and repeating, 'We shot him, we killed Kennedy.' They said the woman wore a polka dot dress."

"Damn, if I hadn't worked such a long shift yesterday, I would have been guarding him tonight."

Schneid had been laying half-asleep on his couch watching a late-night movie when he got the call. As a local police officer, he and other local officers had been assigned to aid Secret Service and the FBI agents guarding Robert Kennedy.

Kennedy had met with Schneid's executive protection detail earlier in the year. He told them how important it was for him to mix with the crowd. He understood that their job was to protect him from the crowd, but he felt it was important for him to mingle with the crowds. He wanted to shake their hands and show his gratitude for their coming out to support him. Schneid noticed that Kennedy's hands were scabbed and bloodied from shaking hands with thousands of people during the campaign. People felt they had to touch him, and he obliged them whenever possible.

"Gentlemen, all the people want to do is touch me, not hurt me."

There had been no credible threats made against Kennedy, so he got his way. Earlier in the year, Schneid had been on

Kennedy's protection detail for a speech at Robbie's Restaurant, a fashionable restaurant and banquet hall on the open-air Pomona Mall. After addressing an outside crowd of around three thousand five hundred people, Kennedy entered Robbie's Restaurant to speak to over four hundred guests at a luncheon sponsored by the Pomona Central Business District Association.

"I understand this is a nonpartisan lunch," Kennedy joked at one point, "so, I'll just say if I was running for office and if I won the California primary, then I'll be able to come back to the Los Angeles County Fair the following September. That's actually why I'm running for president."

The tremendous crowd of people made it difficult for security to keep Kennedy from being crushed. Schneid was inside the two-story restaurant when he encountered a man in his twenties who was slender, about five feet five, dark curly hair and dark-complected. He was with a Caucasian woman, in her twenties, five foot five, slender figure with shoulder-length straight brown hair in a polka dot dress. They were trying to get inside the restaurant's kitchen door.

"Mam, that door is locked, and the kitchen is off-limits to you."

"Oh. Can you tell me which way Senator Kennedy will enter the luncheon?"

"He'll probably go up the main stairs to the second floor."

Several minutes later, Schneid observed the same couple climb over a brick facade adjacent to the stairs and then over a stair railing behind ticket checkers at the foot of the stairs.

Sometime after the assassination, Schneid was interviewed by the FBI. During all public gatherings for candidates, the Bureau had always taken crowd photos for "just in case" reasons. For this case, they had pictures of Schneid doing crowd control inside the restaurant with Sirhan Sirhan near him in the photo.

"Officer Schneid, do you remember this person?"

Unaware of who it was, he told them, "Yes, he was pushing to get closer to Kennedy as he worked his way up the stairs. I had to push him away."

"Where did you first see him?"

"Near the restaurant kitchen door off the lobby. He was with a woman in a polka dot dress."

Sirhan Sirhan admitted to assassinating Kennedy, but to this day, it is unclear as to whether or not he had accomplices, let alone one in a polka dot dress. Audio recordings inside the hotel pantry recording thirteen rounds going off and more bullets were recovered in the wood decorations of the room than the eight Sirhan had in his revolver. None of the protection detail fired their weapons. So, it remains a mystery as to how the assassination actually went down. To make matters even more mysterious, all of the evidence secured that night and locked up in the LAPD evidence locker inexplicably vanished.

From an evidentiary standpoint, it was hard to believe that he was the only one who fired a weapon. To this day, accounting for all of the bullets remains one of the unanswered questions about the Robert F. Kennedy assassination.

Earl's official report about what the couple had told him in the hotel lobby also disappeared, just like the woman in the polka dot dress.

GOOD MORNING AMERICA, DEFEATING BIGOTRY

"Bigotry dwarfs the soul by shutting out the truth."
- Edwin Hubbel Chapin

It was 9:30 a.m. on Schneid's day off when the phone rang.

"Bill, this is Bruce. I just got off the phone with a producer from ABC's *Good Morning America*. They want to know the name of the person who I wrote my L. A. Free Press article about and his contact information. Shall I give them the info.?"

"Why do they want to know who I am?"

"I'm not sure, but it must have something to do with your being a cop with an open mind about women and gays serving on the force."

"Hmm, ok, give them my name and number."

Thirty minutes later, Schneid got another call. "Is this Officer Bill Schneid?"

"Maybe. Who's calling?"

"Sorry, this is Hal Cummings, a producer *with ABC's Good Morning America*. Is this Bill?"

"You can call me Bill. What can I do ya for, Hal?"

"We read a story about you in the L. A. Free Press. We got your name and number from the writer and would like to fly you to our New York studio to do a live debate with an NYPD Commander on whether or not women and homosexuals could function effectively in law enforcement. Would you be willing to do that? We'd fly you here, put you up for the weekend, all on us."

"Who's the Commander?"

"I'm not supposed to tell you. It's better that way."

"Ok, I'll accept if you satisfy a few conditions. You fly me first class and put me up in a five-star hotel."

"No problem."

"Also, you don't use my name and department affiliation a secret, blackout my face, and alter my voice."

"You got it. We've thought of that already. Do you watch the show."

"I do whenever I'm not working."

"Then you know that David Hartman and Sandy Hill will be interviewing you and the Commander."

"One more thing. Although I respect and am open-minded about them, I don't participate in the gay and lesbian scene. I just know a lot about them from working my beats in Los Angeles and Hollywood."

"Ok, point noted."

On the flight to New York from Los Angeles, Schneid mentioned to one of the flight attendants that he would be on the *next day's Good Morning America* but wouldn't say why he would be on it.

The morning of the interview, Schneid was picked up in front of his five-star hotel by a black limousine. To his surprise, the Commander he was to debate was already in the limo.

As soon as they took off, the Commander turned to Schneid and said, "Where did they get you from, Central Casting? I'm looking at you, and I can tell a fag when I see one."

Schneid dropped his baritone voice an octave and humorously replied, "Oh really? Yeah, right, they got me out of Central Casting. I was the only highly educated open-minded cop they could find."

On air, David Hartman read Bill's resume, his background, training, experience and federal medals and commendations for his valor, honor, and accomplishments. Schneid glanced at the Commander. He had turned visibly white, and his jaw had dropped. His initial assessment of Schneid being from Central Casting had been way off.

After the reading the litany of Schneid's law enforcement excellence, the Commander asked, "David, how would you like it if a woman or gay cop was trying to find your missing son?"

"All I would care about is finding my missing son. I don't care who finds him."

And so it went. The misogynistic and homophobic Commander's face got redder and redder as he fumbled to find reasons why women and gays couldn't function well without disrupting their fellow officers. "...they're not strong enough... can't run fast enough... they can be blackmailed... they would adversely affect police morale... they are emotionally unstable... they're not dependable in the field... etc."

Schneid patiently listened to the Commander's diatribe, then "ate" the Commander for breakfast by using evidence and facts to effectively countering the Commander's unsupportable statements. The NYPD would eventually drop its misogynistic and homophobic agenda but not without great internal resistance.

After the show, Schneid spoke to the producer, "I'm done with New York. Book me on the first flight home."

By coincidence, the same flight crew that had brought him there was crewing his return flight. They welcomed him aboard with applause. They had watched him on *Good Morning America* and thought he had won the day.

LOU GRANT, "YOU'RE ONE HELL OF A MAN"

"God grant me the serenity to accept the things I cannot change, the courage to change the things I can, and the wisdom to know the difference."
- Reinhold Niebuhr

Mark ran up the two-story apartment's stairs and ducked into a cleaning closet to wait for the pursuing cop. As the cop approached the closet with gun drawn, Mark flung open its door stunning and knocking the cop's gun loose. Mark got to it first and pointed it point-blank at the officer.

"Now I'm going to do to you the same as I did to my lover last week."

He pulled back the hammer just as Officer Schneid came up the stairs with his gun drawn. Seeing Schneid, Mark turned his gun toward him and fired. Schneid took a hit in his left shoulder as he got off two rounds. Mark flew backward with a bullet in his heart and another in his solar plexus.

Medics came, and the suspect was pronounced dead at the scene. As Schneid sat in the back of an ambulance, his unscathed partner came up to him and said, "Bill, you saved my life. You were there for me. I should never have doubted your abilities to be a cop. After today, you'll always be my fucking hero. You saved my life, and my family will forever be in your debt."

A year later, Schneid looked across the table at Seth Freeman, and said, "So, you want to know how I got my medals of valor and honor?"

The waiter arrived.

Schneid looked up and said, "A Cadillac margarita on the rocks with salt. For dinner, I'll have the Casa Escobar Special."

"And you, Sir?"

"A Cadillac margarita and the Camarones Mojo de Ajo."

Freeman, a writer who worked for Mary Tyler Moore Production Company's *Lou Grant* drama series, turned to Schneid, "To answer your question, yes, that and your acceptance of women and gay cops on the force. Our producers saw you debate the NYPD Commander on *Good Morning America.*

"I get it that my story of saving my partner will make a great episode for your show, but I don't want to face any backlash from my fellows in blue."

"Bill, trust me. We'll do everything in our power to protect your identity. This won't be the first time we've faced this challenge."

After Schneid gave Seth accounts of several harrowing incidents while on undercover and regular duty, Seth decided he would write about the shooting in the apartment house incident.

"We're working on season three, and we want your story to be the first episode."

"So, I take it you want to write about my philosophical differences with the rank and file."

"Right, and you've already given me enough material to write several episodes about your bravery as a cop. But here's the twist. My storyline will be not just about you being an erudite and tolerant cop, but a cop who is misconstrued by his fellow officers as being into the gay scene. From our interview today, I'll write the screenplay. If you don't mind, Roger Young, the director, would also like you to be on set as our tech advisor during filming."

They talked the whole day, and Seth eventually wrote the episode called *Cop*. It became the highest-rated episode of the *Lou Grant's* Emmy Award-Winning series. Joe Penny played Bill as Dave Tynan, a super bright and brave LAPD cop, who was still "in the closet" and concerned that if his fellow bigoted officers found out about his sexuality, they would make his life miserable, if not unbearable.

During the wrap party after the last scene was shot, Joe Penny pulled Schneid aside and said, "Bill, my agent was concerned about me playing a different kind of cop. But I insisted on doing it, and I'm glad I did. Your story is an important one that people need to hear."

Ed Asner, aka, Lou Grant, then came over and threw his arms around Schneid and gave him a big hug. "Bill, you know, you're one hell of a man."

Overwhelmed with gratitude for being acknowledged, Schneid had tears in his eyes as he drove home across town. To this day, they remain friends.

Lou Grant S03E01 Cop

Lou Grant speaks with Joe Penny (aka, Bill Schneid)

HARASSMENT WORKS
BOTH WAYS

The brass was determined to get Schneid off the force.

"Schneid, I'm reassigning you to the traffic division starting today. You'll be riding alone."

"Alright."

Schneid knew Captain Parker was moving him to what everyone thought was a boring division to demean and bore him enough to quit. Instead, Schneid made it a project of fascination and memorized the whole California Vehicle Code and made a note of several sections.

Up to that point, the department's traffic cops hadn't been stopping trucks that were overweight. Schneid would take potentially overweight trucks to the public scales and weigh them. An overweight truck fine was often thousands of dollars. He thought that was not only a great revenue producer for the city, but he was also saving the asphalt roadways from those too-heavy trucks. It also kept him from being bored.

He would check out five or six citation books at a time from his station because he knew he was going to be busy and he didn't want to have to keep going back for more citation books. He was writing so many tickets and bringing in so much revenue it was making all of the other traffic cops look bad.

So, Parker said, " Schneid, your new traffic beat is West Mission Blvd from Highway 71 to Hamilton. Don't go off your beat. I don't want to see a single citation from anywhere outside of that stretch. Comprende?"

"That's only about a mile stretch of road, Captain."

"That's right, Schneid. You got something to say about that?"

"No, Sir. A one mile stretch of road it will be for me. I look forward to it, Sir."

"Get the fuck out of my office, Schneid."

It turns out that that stretch of the boulevard was used by truckers as a short cut, so Schneid ending up writing more tickets on that one-mile stretch of road than he had wandering all over the city.

When Captain Parker found out, he totally lost it.

Schneid was then assigned to the department's first bicycle patrol. He and the other bicycle officers didn't have uniforms like present-day bicycle police. Instead, they wore civilian clothes, like jeans and Pendleton shirts. Trying to stop people wearing civvies had its challenges, but he didn't mind being outside on a bike so much. Then winter set in. It became miserable riding around in the cold and rainy weather eight hours a day.

Schneid sent a memo to Parker, asking, "When the weather gets lousy, would it be alright for us to give up the bicycles and patrol in undercover cars?"

The unsympathetic Parker responded with this comment written on top of Schneid's note: "Dress warmer, peddle faster."

A couple of months later, Schneid got a memo from the Chief, "Officer Schneid, you are hereby suspended for one month without pay for wearing 'sap' gloves while on duty." Sap, or weighted-knuckle gloves, have lead powder stuffed in the knuckle areas to give more force to a slap or fist punch. Schneid had only used them a couple of times to subdue subjects with open-handed forward slaps and never with a closed fist that might have brought unwanted attention to his actions.

Somehow, the Chief heard that Schneid had sap gloves and decided to suspend him for a month. When he got the notice, Schneid checked the Rules and Regulations of the Pomona Police Department and found nothing mentioning sap gloves or anything like them. So, he appealed to the Pomona Police Merit System Commission.

Captain Brooke, who was the Under-Chief, pulled Schneid aside and said, "Are you crazy, you're taking on the Chief?"

"The Chief is wrong. He can't just arbitrarily say this is illegal or against department policy and then suspend me for thirty days based on nothing. Listen, I'm not some hick from Oklahoma like him. He's fucking with the wrong guy."

They appeared before the Merit System Commission. The Chief presented his argument first, and then Schneid gave his. The Merit System Commissioners, a couple of which were Optimist International members, had previous knowledge of the Chief's attempt to make life miserable for Schneid. They conferred and ruled not only in Schneid's favor, but they also ordered the Chief to redo the entire department manual immediately.

THE SQUARE PEG VS THE ROUND HOLE

*"We must always remember that the police
are recruited from the criminal classes."*
- Gore Vidal

It was around one in the morning when Patrol Officer Bill Schneid and his partner spotted a teenager sitting alone in his car by the side of the road. They pulled over and carefully approached the boy's car from behind.

"Young man, why are you parked here at this hour? What's the problem?"

"I'm out of gas, Sir, and don't have any money, and I can't get my parents on the phone."

"Well, we can't leave you here alone. Hop in. We've got a gas can in the trunk. We'll drive you to a gas station and then bring you back here."

"But I don't have any money."

Schneid reached into his wallet and pulled out a five-dollar bill. "Here, this should buy enough gas to get you home."

"Thank you, Sir. Thank you so much!"

Schneid's partner looked at him, "You're a fool. You really think you'll ever see that money back?"

"It doesn't matter. I'm loaning him the money and whether or not I get it back is up to his morals. Meanwhile, I want to help this kid get home."

It was worth the five bucks to Schneid, but his cynic partner couldn't understand that. A month later, Schneid's name was called out during roll call, "Schneid, you have an envelope."

Schneid opened it and found five bucks inside and a long thank you note from the kid. He showed it to his "asshole" partner. "You got lucky." Nothing would change this cop's mind.

Schneid's psychiatrist asked, "You say you see the writing on the wall with the force. What do you mean by that?"

"I'm the proverbial square peg trying to fit into a round hole. Aside from my lieutenant, I'm not like the other cops in the force. I'm single. I like art and gourmet food, I don't beat up people for questioning or resisting me, I don't hate Blacks, Chicanos, and people who don't look like me, and I don't hate people in general. I get off helping people."

"And you didn't know what most police officers are like before you went into the force?"

"No, I guess I didn't fully understand what makes these cops tick."

"I recall you being elated to get back into the department."

"Yeah, after doing five years of undercover, it felt great to finally be a regular cop with regular patrol duties."

"So, you're saying that cops are too prejudicial, but isn't their job to judge and profile people during their regular duties?"

"Yes, but not to the degree I'm witnessing daily. Remember, law enforcement is mostly made up of cops who were blue-collar worker kids. Their parents and community teach them racial and ethnic intolerance from day one. They are not of the intelligentsia, and they are not sophisticated. They're close-minded, and they believe what they want to believe no matter how off-base or idiotic it is and they hold grudges toward anybody who confronts them on their shit.

"They grow up fairly powerless. Dad drive's a tow truck and being a cop is their first chance at not being yelled at by their parents. As cops, they have the power they were never allowed to have grown up. Boy, I see that all the time, especially when they arrest some guy by first taking him down to the ground and start beating him up. I watch incredulously, thinking, 'Why are you beating this guy up? He didn't do anything to justify that.'

"I'm always amazed at the level of violence behind the badge for no reason. You meet force with force, and if there's no reason, why beat the shit out of somebody just because he cussed you out.

"Remember, I didn't come from a blue-collar family. I grew up hanging around intellectuals, who were open-minded people."

"How do you handle verbal abuse?"

"Listen, I've been called a Pig plenty of times. I always respond with a smile on my face and an "oink-oink." Being called that amuses me. I don't take it as personal, and I don't respond with a, 'You're going to pay for that!' But so many cops do.

"I didn't realize it until I worked inside the department after doing undercover work that I was dealing with a bunch of uneducated, angry morons. That's the main reason they hate my lieutenant who befriended me because he's an artist, is bright, has a bachelor's degree in English and always corrects their ill-written reports with a red pen."

"Oh, my. That must really set them off."

"Yeah, he's poison to them because he has some brains, and you just don't belong if you have brains."

"As an undercover agent assigned to various task force duties, have you seen this lack of empathy in other enforcement agencies?"

"On the local levels, yes and it's worse in some parts of the country than in others. On the federal level, less so."

"What I'm hearing is not very comforting."

"Look at it like this. It requires a certain type of mindset. It's an occupation very much akin to the military. So someone asks you why you want to join the military today?"

"Oh, to protect our country."

"From whom? No one is going to invade us. We're at a nuclear standoff with the Soviets. So in my mind, nothing justifies joining the military in peacetime unless you want to be a badass and shoot people."

"Or you want the medical insurance and the G.I. Bill benefits."

"Yes, the benefits. Excellent point and that's why you should join the Coast Guard. When's the last time a Coastguardsman got shot?

"It's the mentality.' No, I want to join the Marines.'

'Oh, why do you want to join the Marines?'

'Because I can be a badass, that's why. In real life, I'm not.'"

"It's the same with most cops.

'Boy, I want that badge and that gun so I can stop anybody at any time.'"

"They get a rush out of it. I see it all the time."

"And you don't?"

"Listen, I killed a lot of people in Southeast Asia. I did that because they trained me to do it. I did things for the good of the cause, as I perceived it. It was a war zone. We're not in a war zone here. I don't want to hurt or kill anyone unless I absolutely have to. I'm done with that."

"That's good to hear."

"Look, I wanted to be a cop because I thought I could make a difference. Now, I feel like I'm not going anywhere, and morons surround me. I'm not one of the boys and don't want to be."

"So, Bill, where are you headed with this?"

"I'm getting fed up going out on calls and doing work with these guys. I want to get myself into something more challenging, where I can make a difference."

"And where would that be?"

With a smirk, Schneid replied, "I thought you would never ask. I'm thinking of leaving the force to freelance for federal agencies where I can use my experience and sleuth-like mind."

THE PRICE OF A POLICE BADGE

"There is no 'u' in tacos."
- Captain Wallick

"Fine, I'll take the taco."

Officer Schneid had repeatedly tried to pay the taco shop owner the thirty-nine cents for the taco but the owner, grateful to see a police unit around in his crime-ridden neighborhood, wouldn't take payment. When Schneid tried to pay, the owner followed him back to his cruiser and threw the coins into the car.

Officer Schneid was hungry, and this was the only place to eat on his beat, and official policy dictated that he wasn't to go off his beat and out of the city for food. So, he gave up trying to pay and drove off with the free taco. The other problem was that an Internal Affairs (I.A.) officer was doing a routine ride-along with Schneid.

The I.A. officer filed a beefed-up report with Internal Affairs accusing Schneid of accepting a gratuity, which was against department policy. Schneid got called before the I.A. Captain.

"Captain Wallick, it was a judgment call. I tried to pay the guy, but he refused. I wasn't going to throw the money back at him. I got tired of arguing with him, so, yes, I took the thirty-nine cent taco."

"Well, you know we have a gratuity policy."

"Right, but didn't the department recently announce that a local men's store would give us 10% off if we showed our police id.? Isn't that a gratuity?"

"Well, that's different."

"Well, I don't understand. Explain to me how that's different.
"

"Well, it just is. Now I want to know the name of every police officer that's been accepting gratuities at that taco shop."

"You're not going to get that from me."

"Okay, then you're suspended for a week without pay."

There was silence in the room. Then the Captain finally said, "What do you think of that?"

Schneid snapped back, "I should have ordered fries with it."

The next day, Schneid walked in and slammed his badge on the Captain's desk, then cleared out his locker. "Captain, here, you can have my twenty-nine cent shield and put it where the sun don't shine." As he started to walk out, a sergeant high-fived him and said, "Thanks, Schneid for not saying anything about the rest of us taking free tacos." The department would continue to get free tacos.

So, Schneid ended his four-plus years as a patrol officer with the force.

AS A FREELANCE
FEDERAL AGENT

After almost nine years as a police officer, five of them as an undercover cop, Schneid became a freelance federal secret agent operating across the globe in units with skill sets similar to those of elite Navy Seal and Delta Force units.

Due to national security concerns, not included in this book are most of his units' operational activities. With government approval, we may be able to write about them in a sequel to this book. However, the 2006 to 2009 television series "The Unit" was about him and his units' operations. His assignments were secretive, far-reaching and wide-ranging, requiring high-security clearances, often with directives straight from the White House.

Eventually, his high-level security clearances allowed high-ranking government officials to engage him for unusual high-level consultations dealing with the War on Drugs and UFO alien sequesters. The following stories show the breadth of his experiences during the longest period of his life.

PABLO ESCOBAR
TERRITORY, COLOMBIA

"I'm a decent man who exports flowers."
- Pablo Escobar

Coca flowers

Agent Schneid kneeled in the sizeable tropical mountain clearing as the early morning mist floated around him. Carlos, his translator, emerged running out of the trees. "Señor, you've been found out. The cartel no longer believes you are a legitimate buyer. The meeting is just a scam, and they're holding agents Arias and Samuel. They're planning to kidnap and kill you."

Schneid pulled out his encrypted satcom phone and called to his handler for immediate extraction. No reply. He kept trying when twelve members of the cartel entered the far side of the clearing dragging federal agents Arias and Samuel with them. The six guards had shotguns, and AK-47's and the lieutenants had handguns. Cautiously, they spread out around the edges of the clearing.

He shut off the satcom. "Stay down low in the grass, Carlos. They haven't spotted us yet."

Part of a joint federal narcotics task force, Schneid had been parachuted into the jungle two weeks earlier to meet with and arrange a big cocaine buy. His cover was that he was a Jewish-American Syndicate buyer from Los Angeles. At first, things had gone well, but the six Pablo Escobar cartel lieutenants he had met with weren't stupid. They were cautious and told him they would get back to him after they had vetted him. Somehow, they had found out he was an undercover agent for one of the American law enforcement agencies. He didn't think it was Carlos because some of Escobar's men had raped two of his primas or cousins.

The head cartel honcho, Luis, was the first to spot them. "Allí están! Mátalos!"

"Carlos, we need to split up. Head for the trees."

The guards started firing as they ran. Bullets zinged by his ears. Then he felt two burning hits in his left thigh. Another bullet grazed his shoulder, and another hit his lower chest. He could still move but no longer fast enough. He wouldn't make it to the trees, and even if he did, this was their territory, so he knew it was only time before they would catch up to him.

As he ran, he pulled out two 40 caliber Glocks with sub-projectile ammo from his underarm holsters. The six soldiers were closing in on him. He thought to himself, "I'm not going to make it to the trees, and if I did, they could easily hunt me down."

So, he stopped, spun around, weaved his way toward them and opened fire. Surprised by his boldness, the six gunmen briefly stopped firing. He took advantage of their hesitation and began the killing. After Southeast Asia, he and his unit had trained with the Mossad for such situations. His ambidextrous aim from several positions was deadly. Within seconds, he had killed or mortally wounded all six gunmen. The six lieutenants retreated with their two captives and took up defensive positions in the trees, but Schneid didn't stop.

He knew the lieutenants were lousy shots, but one of them managed to hit him in his upper left arm. Still, he limped toward them, dodging their bullets. After killing two of the lieutenants, the other four, wounded, gave up and threw down their pistols.

"Carlos, get your ass over here!"

Carlos emerged from the trees across the clearing. "Be right there, Señor, as soon as I change my pants! Holy shit, I hope you never get mad at me."

Arias and Samuelson were in bad shape from being tortured. After Carlos tied up the lieutenants, Schneid finally got through to his handler on the satcom. Within twenty minutes, a chopper arrived at the clearing and extracted Schneid, Carlos, the two agents and four of the still-living lieutenants. Wanted fugitives, the four cartel members, ended up in U.S. custody and Schneid ended up in a military hospital for a series of surgeries. To this day, he doesn't know what happened to the Cartel members that he delivered. For his efforts, he secretly received federal departmental Law Enforcement Medals of Honor and Valor.

THE WORLD BANK
EXECUTIVE

"Having lost sight of our objectives we need to re-
double our efforts."
- anonymous

"If this is truly a war on drugs, why don't we just send in our Marines and these people would be history tomorrow?"

Everyone around the conference table looked at Lt. Colonel Schneid like he was crazy.

"Seriously, are we just playing at this, or are we going to get down to business? We're losing good people and I recently almost got killed in Colombia on a mission."

Top law enforcement officials from several American intelligence agencies and top officials from the World Bank gathered in New York for briefings on drug cartel impacts on the United States, money laundering and current joint anti-drug task force operations.

The World Bank's "elder statesman" with silver hair looked at Schneid and said, "Son, let me explain something you obviously don't know about our war on drugs. First, let me ask you if you have a clue just how much the Colombian government owes the U.S. banking system?"

"No, I don't."

"Well, let me put it this way. If all the Juan Valdez's, the coffee plantation guys, who are also growing coca, go out of business, we would never get paid back any of the money Colombia owes us. And Son, they owe us a lot of money. If these Colombians' sole business is growing coffee beans and not coca, our banks won't get paid back."

"So you're telling me that we basically can't afford to wipe out the cocaine business and win this drug war?"

"You know, you're one smart shit."

"That's just unbelievable. In other words, to protect our banking system, we do just token enforcement to help Colombia pay back the money that they owe our banks."

"As I said, Son, you're one smart shit."

JUST A FLEA ON AN ELEPHANT'S ASS

"You can get the monkey off your back, but the
circus never leaves town."
- Anne Lamott

"Holy shit, will you look at those ceiling-high stacks of cocaine and currency. This is what it must have been like for Howard Carter's archeology team when they entered Pharaoh Tutankhamen's tomb full of treasures in 1921." It was beyond their wildest dreams. This was the biggest haul any of the agents had ever seen.

After the last round had been fired and the surviving suspects rounded up, Schneid began to assess what was in the 3,500 square foot Sylmar, California warehouse rented by the Colombian cartel. Schneid and his team had just blasted their way into the warehouse. The initial investigation started when a snitch told authorities there would be a shipment of pure cocaine coming into the Port of Los Angeles inside a container on a specific cargo ship.

When one of their dogs alerted them, DEA agents working with Customs officers found the cocaine on board the ship inside a dozen full-sized oxygen tanks stuffed with cocaine inside a large container. 99.9% pure cocaine filled the tanks.

A tactical decision was made to leave the shipment alone,

not to tell anyone and not to make a bust until they located its destination. A truck picked up the container and left the port. It was followed by a high-altitude helicopter as it wound its way through Los Angeles. Only Schneid and his eight men knew of the surveillance because of the concern for inside agency leaks. His veteran DEA-led special task force unit had worked together on countless operations.

When the truck arrived at a warehouse disguised as an import business, more than a dozen armed men came out of the warehouse. They used a large crane to offload the cargo container and put it into the warehouse.

The surveillance team called for immediate backup. Their backup elite force used tactics that would make any SEAL and SWAT team members proud, if not envious. Now, civilians, almost all had been members of special mission teams such as LRRPs, SEAL Team 6 and Delta Force. They were a fearless unit immune to anything and armed with the most advanced close-combat military weaponry available. Unlike SWAT and SEAL units who often had extended downtime, they were always on missions, sometimes several a week. They knew and trusted each other trust with their lives.

They played for keeps because they knew that the minute they entered the warehouse, the shit would hit the fan, and it did. They knew the cartel members would fight with their lives because their wives and children were being held hostage in Mexico and Colombia. If they lost part or all of the shipment, their relatives would be beheaded or killed. They were more afraid of the cartel than any U.S. agents. Schneid and his unit knew from experience that they were in for a horrific firefight.

Bam-bam-bam. Flash-bang grenades went into the warehouse first, and then they entered and lit it up like the 4th of July. The team hit them with withering and accurate firepower from their assault rifles and pistols. The well-armed cartel members fought back, but they were overwhelmed within minutes.

None of his team got killed, and only one was slightly

wounded, but six cartel members lost their lives and most of the rest wounded. First, to go in and shooting with both hands, Schneid killed three of the six with his two 40 caliber Glocks.

The drugs and cash were cataloged and confiscated by personnel in scrub suits with no pockets or places to stash and conceal any drugs or money. Closed-circuit TV's set up inside the warehouse recorded the counting of cash and drugs. It took the collection team days to do all of the countings of coke and money. It was the most massive drug bust in the history of the United States. Along with the cocaine-filled oxygen tanks, thousands of one-kilo packages of cocaine were found stored in boxes among piñatas and velvet canvas paintings. They removed twenty-one and a half tons of cocaine, along with twelve million dollars in cash, mostly in twenty and one hundred dollar bills. The street value of the cocaine was $6 billion. The raid on the warehouse shocked even veteran law enforcement officials.

According to ledgers and documents seized, most of the cocaine came in through El Paso, then over a ribbon of concrete and asphalt through New Mexico and Arizona before arriving at the warehouse in Sylmar, California.

The cartel involved took a hit that would have bankrupted a healthy business, but it was just a bump in the road for it. Their cost to grow, produce, and distribute was pennies on the dollar compared to what they lost in retail value from the bust. Their profit margin potential remained so huge that they could suffer those kinds of losses and not even blink an eye.

The Sylmar bust that day made headlines in the U.S., but ultimately, it was just a flea on this elephant's ass.

LUNCH WITH ALIENS
@ AREA 51

*"If the government is covering up knowledge
of aliens, they are doing a better job of it
than they do at anything else."*
- Stephen Hawking

Lt. General Cheney of NORAD command put his foot on his desk, leaned back in his cushy chair and spoke into the secure landline, "Hey, Bill, how the hell are you? I heard you had a rough but successful time in South America."

"Yeah, the thing turned upside on me, but I'm on the heal. I still have a cartel souvenir in my back a bit too close to my spine for the docs to take out."

"Sorry about that. Listen, I hear you're in Vegas. Wanna come up tomorrow to Area 51 for lunch and a little schmoozing?"

"I haven't been up there for years. What's up. Why have lunch way up there?"

"There's something I want you to see."

"Ok, I'll drive up and be there by noon."

Schneid pulled off old SR 25, now called SR 375 onto a nameless dirt road and headed west past various military restricted area warning signs and miles of Joshua Trees. About eleven miles in, he was met by well-armed MP's in two jeeps.

"Sir, are you aware that you've entered into a restricted area?"

"I am and am expected by Lt. General Cheney. Here's my identification."

They radioed in his information, and seconds later, the MP's waived and said, "Lt. Colonel Schneid, you are cleared to proceed." Three checkpoints later, he pulled up to HQ where the three-star General greeted him.

"Great to see you, Bill. I hope the boys were polite to you on the way in."

"Hah! Nothing but cordial. So, what's up? Why are we here for lunch?"

"Patience, my friend. Before we have lunch, I want you to see something out of this world, literally."

They climbed into a jeep, and a driver took them to a site called S-4, a few miles south of the base. After enduring several checkpoints requiring biometric fingerprint checks and identification card verifications, they arrived at a hangar surrounded by armed guards that were big enough to hold a 747. In the middle of the hangar was a tungsten-gray craft on an elevated platform surrounded by people in white jumpsuits. The ship was more oblong than round, about twelve feet high and twenty feet long with two narrow horizontal windows wrapped around one end.

"Wow, what have we here? Is this some new recon craft from the Skunk Group?"

"Oh no, Bill, this isn't of our making. This is a bona fide alien spaceship, a UFO."

"Yeah right, and piloted by little green men."

"Well, you're not far off about their color."

"Are you shittin me?"

"No, come take a look a closer look at this thing, and then I'll introduce you to its alien pilots."

"Where'd you find this thing?"

"Can't tell ya. Classified, above your level."

Slowly, they walked around the craft. On one side was a sealed oblong opening. At least, Schneid figured it was an opening because he could make out a very thin line in its fuselage around it.

"Where's the front end?"

"We're not sure. There's no visible damage anywhere. We found it partially buried at the end of an extended crash crater. So, it was going pretty fast when it hit."

"No damage from impact. Amazing. Any clue as to why it crashed?"

"Not so far."

"Maybe it ran out of fuel."

"Bill, we have no idea. At this point, we are clueless."

They walked around to the other side, and the general pointed out a vertical line of hieroglyphic-like symbols.

"Have you been able to decipher any of this?"

"Not yet but we've got top cryptologists and archaeologists working on it."

They stood and gazed at it for a while. Then walked over to where scientists had scrapped off surface material from the fuselage.

"We've got the best metallurgists and atomic scientists trying to figure out what material they used to make it. It doesn't match up with anything on our atomic chart, so we think it's made from some unknown interstellar element."

"Could it be of biological origin?"

"Haven't considered that. That's why I thought it a good idea to have you come up here and have a look. You always have something to add to the equation."

The general turned to his aide-de-camp, "Captain, let's task some of the biologists to examine this thing. Pronto!" The Captain spun on his heels and took off.

"Ok, Bill, want to take a look inside?"

"You bet."

They climbed into to find a single large space with no furniture, like an unfurnished house. Spread around its sides and ceiling were hundreds of tiny colored flashing light arrays, with a concentration of them in a panel situated between two two-foot by twelve-foot horizontal rectangular windows of an unknown transparent material.

"We think the area between those two windows is the control and command center, but as you can see, there's no writing or symbols of any kind anywhere in here."

"How do they fly this thing?"

"No clue. We can't make heads or tails out of this light panel or any of the light arrays."

"I don't see any galley, sleeping, or bathroom areas. How the hell did they dine, sleep, and shit in this thing? If this is the control center, there's nothing to sit on in front of it."

"Yep, nothing about it has any rhyme or reason, at least nothing that we can relate to."

"Yeah, I see what you mean. There's no knobs or levers, just these little lights. Have you figured out the power source of all these lights and its source of propulsion?"

"Working on it. At this point, we can't even figure out how it would take off. Far as I know, it might lift-off straight up."

"I take it you've also found no exhaust system."

"Correct. No apparent exhaust system or exhaust outlets anywhere."

"This is some crazy shit."

"You got that right. Everyone's imagination is running wild. This thing is way beyond us. Its technology is super advanced."

Schneid was starting to get a queasy feeling in his stomach. He felt like he was on the downswing of a rollercoaster ride. "Stonehenge and Easter Island are baffling enough but General, this takes the cake."

They finished their inside tour and walked out of the hanger and into an adjacent high-security room cold enough to be a freezer. Inside were two aliens in separate hermetically-sealed transparent plastic cubicles surrounded by people in white biohazard suits. The aliens didn't look like typical science fiction aliens. They were about three feet high, greenish-gray gelatinous blobs with no distinguishable appendages like arms, legs, noses or heads and no openings like eyes, mouths or gills.

"Look at that. This one's outer surface appears to be flowing. Its surface simultaneously recycles itself inwards and outwards. Kinda reminds me of a slimy dark slinky going downstairs, then somehow going back up. Weird, and their color, it's nauseating."

"Are they dead or alive?"

"We think the one you're looking at is alive and the other one deceased, but we're not entirely sure about that either. It might be in a dormant state."

"Except for the active surface on this one, they pretty much look the same to me."

"Yeah, looks that way to me but the scientists are saying otherwise. They've been kinda touching and poking them with instruments. This one responds by quivering, but the other one doesn't respond at all. Notice its surface isn't moving like the surface on the other one."

"Well, now it makes sense as to why there are no levers or buttons inside their spaceship. They have no appendages with which to move anything. Maybe they operate things via mental power. Do you know whether or not they have brains or a nervous system?"

"The necropsy team will determine that soon enough.

They're scheduled to dissect the dead one."

"What are you planning to do with the live one?"

"Love to tell you, Bill, but then I'd have to..."

"...I know. Shoot me."

"What about the dead one?"

"Come on. Now you're asking me to shoot you twice."

"Ok, ok. I get it. Just let me ask you this. What happens if and when the public finds out?"

"My superiors figure that after the initial shock, the public would learn to live with the truth. If that happens, it actually might cause Congress to increase our military budget. The main reason we've got this so hush-hush is to keep the Soviets or Chinese from getting hold of any alien technology. Imagine, if we can figure this whole alien thing out, we'll have an unbeatable technological edge on the Commies, and everyone else for that matter."

As they watched, scientists continued to work with the two aliens. A table was set up for lunch in the observation area. Schneid and the general both drank iced tea, and the general devoured a Cobb salad. Schneid, who had completely lost his appetite, just sat and thought about what he had just witnessed.

"General, this has turned out to be one crazy wild-ass visit."

"Yes, it has."

THE GENERAL'S WOMEN

*"Whoever has experienced the power and
the unrestrained ability to humiliate another human
being automatically loses his own sensations.
Tyranny is a habit, it has its own organic life,
it develops finally into a disease.
The [disease] can kill and coarsen the very best man or woman
to the level of a beast."*
- Fyodor Dostoyevsky

A phone call awoke Schneid in the middle of the night. He rolled over and picked up the receiver of his secure government line. "Schneid here. How may I be of help?"

At the other end was the CIA Baghdad Station Chief.

"Colonel Schneid, Lloyd Everett, Company Station Chief, Baghdad here. We're outside Baghdad and have a problem I'm hoping you might help us. We have a situation with an uncooperative domestic general who we know has been giving Intel to a Sunni insurgent group that's been giving us lots of problems. There's more."

"Yep. Listening."

"Secretary Panetta was just here, and he's shut down some of our interrogation methods. Listen, I'm at the end of my rope, and we have a strong need to stop a pending insurrection field action. Our general knows all but isn't telling. Sir, got any ideas?"

"How much time do you have to extract information?"

"Little to none, Sir."

A brief pause, then, "Is he Shia or Sunni?"

"Shia."

"Ok. Can you bring in his family? Forget the sons, bring in only the wife and daughters."

"We already have the wife and all three daughters in-house."

"Good. Now listen up. Secure the ladies tightly, line them up facing the general. Bring a couple well-endowed G.I.'s and have them strip down to their skivvies. Inform the general that unless he tells you everything you want to know and then some, he and his wife will soon watch his daughters being double-penetrated by the G.I.'s starting with his oldest daughter, then the younger ones with the wife saved for last. Are you following me?"

"Yes, Sir, all of it."

"Well, not to worry about the general. He will talk before the guys can whip out their little weenies. By tradition, a disgraced Shia father is obligated to kill his daughters and maybe his wife if they have been double-deflowered."

After a short pause, "Ok, will give it a try. I'll let you know how it went. Thank you, Sir."

Schneid put the receiver down and tried to get back into his last dream.

Two hours later, the secure line rang again. "Schneid here. How may I be of assistance?"

"It worked, and the ladies are still virgins. Sir, you are the man of the day."

"Great to be of service. Have an excellent day, night, or whatever it is there."

Schneid's years of clandestine field operations had taught him that the end sometimes justified the means, even when it came to threatening the innocent families of targets. Unlike some men, he never let it affect how he slept. Like the soldier he once was, he did whatever it took to get the job done. In this case, Schneid was 99%

sure that the General would not allow his women to be deflowered.

9/11, NATIONAL SECURITY VS A TREADMILL

On September 11, 2001, at 6:37 a.m., San Francisco Field Division Special Agent In Charge (SFSAC) Joe Tejada was huffing and puffing on a treadmill at the 24 Hour Fitness gym on Van Ness Avenue when he got a call on his cell phone.

"Joe here."

"Joe, Bill Schneid in L. A. Have you seen what's happened in New York City?"

"No, I'm in the gym and haven't heard anything from my office. What's up?"

"Two big commercial jets going high velocity have hit New York's two tallest skyscrapers in the World Trade Center. Joe, it's got to be a terrorist attack. They've already tried to bring those buildings down with explosives."

"Holy shit. How many injured and killed?"

"Don't know yet, probably thousands, but security details at every potential strategic or symbolic West Coast target, including Hoover and Glen Canyon Dams on the Colorado River, need to prepare for any additional attacks."

"Yeah, there are a lot of targets of opportunity, including the Golden Gate Bridge.

Bill, you won't believe who's on the treadmill next to me. It's Peter Black, Agent in Charge of the San Fran FBI Field Office who also heads up the S. F. Joint Terrorism Task Force. Hold the line. I'll let him know what's going on."

Less than a minute later, Joe tells Bill, "Ok, I'm on my way to my office. When I told Peter about the attack and our fears for out here, you know what he said? 'As soon as I finish my work-out, I'll head to my office.' Can you believe that?"

"You've got to be kiddin me."

"Swear to God. Bill, how the hell did you, in L. A., know about this before we did?"

"Friends in the right places."

"Well, a huge thanks to you for alerting us and let's keep in touch as this unfolds."

"Important structural challenges remain to be addressed in order to improve the flow of information and to en-hance the FBI's counterterrorism effectiveness..."
- *9/11 Commission Report.*

AS AN UNDERCOVER AGENT & CRIMINOLOGIST

Schneid's undercover drug operations took a toll on his health, but it also encouraged him to study and get a doctorate in criminology with a specialty in drug addiction. As a recognized criminologist with street experience, he was often called to testify in court as a drug expert.

At the same time, he designed court-approved drug rehabilitation programs for young drug addicts and continued to take on freelance undercover assignments for various federal law enforcement and intelligence agencies. Along the way, he occasionally discovered corruption within police forces while doing undercover work, resulting in him having to deal with the politics of corruption that sometimes led to cover-ups or retaliation.

HEROIN WITH A PISTOL AT YOUR HEAD

*"Reality is just a crutch for people
who can't handle drugs."*
- Robin Williams

The heroin dealer put his 45 caliber pistol to Schneid's head and said, "Shoot up, then this deal is done. If you tell me you're allergic to it or some other kind of shit, I'll assume you're a cop and blow your head off."

"No problem. Just keep your finger off the trigger."

Schneid tied off his bicep and plunged the needle deep into a vein. The familiar warm rush crept up his arm, and then he felt the pleasure rush inside his brain. Schneid sat back on the couch and started to sweat and itch. Soon he had the sensation this his body was made of liquid. For twenty minutes, euphoria controlled his being as his body released large amounts of dopamine. For almost four hours, he laid on the couch in a state of drowsiness.

The naive defense attorney approached the jury, then spun around and asked the expert witness, "Well, Detective Schneid, what makes you a drug expert?"

"I've used virtually all of them. Heroin, multiple times over five years."

You could hear a pin drop in the courtroom.

"Detective Schneid, are you aware you're admitting to a felony?"

"I'm not admitting to anything. I'm saying I used those drugs, but I didn't say where or when."

The attorney swallowed and said, "Ok, let's move on."

At the end of one extended stint as an undercover cop, Schneid tried to check himself into a hospital to clean up his system of all of the drugs he had to use in front of drug dealers so as not to get killed. Five years of drug use had taken its toll.

"Hello, Beverly Hills Medical Center. How may I help you?"

"I'm addicted to heroin and want to kick the habit."

"Sir, who is your referral doctor?"

"I don't have one."

"One moment, please."

"Sir, I'm afraid you must have a referral from a doctor to use our facility."

Undeterred, Schneid called other clinics but got similar answers. He got hold of a drug counselor who recommended Dr. Fitzsimmons, who was a leading authority on opiate addiction at the Beverly Hills center, but this time he took a different tack.

"Hello, Beverly Hills Medical Center. How may I help you?"

"This is Dr. Schneid. Is Dr. Fitzsimmons available?"

"No, Sir, Dr. Fitzsimmons is attending a convention in San Francisco."

"I need to get in touch with him as soon as possible. I'm dealing with a patient who is in a life-threatening condition, and I need his advice."

"One moment, Doctor, I will try to reach him."

"Hi, this is Dr. Fitzsimmons. To whom am I speaking?"

Dr. Fitzsimmons patiently listened to Schneid's story.

"Officer Schneid, I'm not used to getting calls from addicts wanting to get off opiates. You're the first."

"Listen, Dr. Fitzsimmons. I've been turned down by your clinic and others already. Would you please make an exception and help me out?"

"I tell you what, let's meet next Monday when I return, and I'll see what I can do to get you admitted."

Dr. Fitzsimmons got Schneid admitted. Recovery was tough for him. Not only did he have to suffer physical and psychological hardships of withdrawal, but he also had to endure the relatively poor hospital food and odious group therapy sessions. Undaunted, he soon found a way to manipulate his way out of both problems.

Just before one of his group therapy sessions, a Rabbi came to the rehab floor of the hospital. A nurse got on the public address system and announced, "Patients, there's a Rabbi here. Does anyone want to see the Rabbi?"

Seeing an opportunity he couldn't pass up, Schneid yelled out, "I do!"

The Rabbi came into Schneid 's room. "How are things going for you, Bill?"

"You know, Rabbi, I have a problem."

"What's that?"

"I'm off of my kosher diet here."

"You were on a kosher diet?"

"I was on one until I came to the hospital."

Schneid had never been on a kosher diet, and he wasn't a practicing Jew.

"Well, we can't have that. I will contact the head of dietary."

The next day, staff presented Schneid with a menu from the famous Canter's delicatessen. Every day after that, they gave him a choice of anything on the menu. Soon, the head of dietary was freaking out because suddenly the food expenses had become ridiculous as Schneid kept ordering expensive food off the Canter's menu. Of course, Schneid was generous with the other patients and often shared his food with them.

One day, he got called into Dr. Fitzsimmons' office. "Bill, we have a problem."

"What's that?"

"The whole floor wants to convert to Judaism."

"The Rabbi must be ecstatic."

His recovery experience of going through the withdrawals and general misery that an addict goes through gave him a new perspective on substance abuse. After he got out of the hospital, he decided to pursue the field of addiction at UCLA. He eventually did his interning and residency at Beverly Hills Medical Center under the tutelage of Dr. Fitzsimmons.

Years later, Dr. Fitzsimmons was found dead on the floor of his Beverly Hills office. Although he died from a drug overdose, he had kept his addiction hidden. His physician and friend who signed the death certificate discovered the actual cause of death, but to protect his reputation, declared that Fitzsimmons had died from a heart attack.

[Note: The Beverly Hills Medical Center is now a hotel. Other medical facilities now use the name.]

THE ARYAN BROTHERHOOD

*"You can tell a lot about a civilization by the quality of
the people found in its jails."*
- David Gerrod

"Hi, I'm Dr. Schneid."
"My Aryan Brotherhood call me Big Mac."
"When was our appointment?"
"Two o'clock."

"It's two-thirty."

"I understand that, but I had to get searched, and they had to find people to bring me up here and all that took time."

"You don't understand."

"What do you mean?"

"When was our appointment?"

"I told you at two o'clock."

"It's two-thirty."

"I understand that, but it was unavoidable."

"Marshall, come over here."

"Yes, Sir."

"Why was Dr. Schneid late?"

"I think you heard him explain why. By the time he gets processed and brought up here, well, these things take time."

"Do you remember when our appointment was?

"Yes, it was at two o'clock."

"It's now past two-thirty."

"Well, Sir, I'm sorry, but that's just the way things are."

"I want to speak to the Lieutenant."

"He's having lunch."

"Apparently, you didn't hear what I just said. I want to speak to the Lieutenant."

"One moment, Sir. I'll get him."

Maybe ten minutes later, the Lieutenant came in wiping his mouth.

"Yes, Sir. What seems to be the problem?"

"Dr. Schneid had a two o'clock appointment with me, and he didn't arrive until two-thirty."

"I want you to look into it and find out why he was detained. I want you to report back to me by four o'clock."

"Yes, Sir. I'll look into it."

"Now, I want all the Marshalls out of the room while I talk to Dr. Schneid in private."

"Yes, Sir. Dr. Schneid, we'll be right outside. Shout if you need us."

Schneid sat there shaking my head in disbelief and thought,

"Here's this guy with his wrists attached to a chain around his waist and his ankles shackled ordering guards and the lieutenant around and them answering to him with 'Yes-Sir's,' and 'No-Sir's.'"

Michael Patrick McElhiney, tall, muscular and covered in tattoos, was a ranking member of the Aryan Brotherhood. For decades it was the most murderous criminal organization in the country. Then "Big Mac" authorities transferred him to the high-security Metropolitan Detention Center in downtown L.A. He was there to face RICO charges for participation in the commission of murders, narcotics trafficking, male prostitution, and gambling.

"So, Big Mac, why did you ask for me?"

"Because I know your reputation and you're the only one I feel I can trust."

"You can, but first I want to ask you a few questions?"

"Well, it depends."

"There's this rumor about how one gets into the A.B.'s. How do you get into it?"

"Dr. Schneid, part of the legend is that you have to kill a Black guy but that's not true at all. You don't get into the Brotherhood unless we invite you in."

"I know your reputation. You've been in incarceration or custody since you were ten years old. You're in your fifties now, incarcerated in one of the hardest-ass prisons in the country. You're going to spend the rest of your life there."

"It's not so bad."

"What do you mean, it's not so bad?"

"Let me explain it this way. When I got moved to USP Marion, Illinois in the '80s, one of the first things I did was to ask for a meeting with the warden. We sat down in a meeting, and I said to the warden, 'I'll make you a deal. If you allow us to control prostitution and narcotics in here, you will never have a fight break out in Marion, IL.' The warden said, 'I'll get back to you.'

"The next day, I got called into the warden's office. He put out his hand and said, 'About your offer yesterday, you've got a deal.'

So, I get everything I want. I get smokes, good food, and we control in-house prostitution, gambling, and narcotics. Ever since we made the deal, there hasn't been a significant fight in Marion, IL."

Schneid thought to himself, "Fuck me. So this is how things work on the inside."

"So now let me ask you this question. Why did you want me here?"

Big Mac reached into his jumpsuit and pulled out this multi-folded piece of paper, folded maybe a hundred times. He proceeded to unfold it like a magician doing a magic trick. This little piece of paper unfolded to be an eight by ten paper.

"Here," and he handed Schneid the paper.

It was handwritten with a pencil in a font so small that Schneid was amazed at how anybody could write it, let alone read it. He needed to use a magnifying glass.

He called out to the Marshalls. "Please get me a magnifying glass." He got Schneid a magnifying glass. On the paper were names, addresses and phone numbers of federal judges, federal prosecutors, FBI agents, and many others in the justice system.

"You may not believe this, but in the Brotherhood, we have a code of honor. Now, I know you've probably heard that we order killings and we orchestrate drug trafficking outside of the prison. Some of that may be true, but we still have a code of honor. I want you to know that this list of Feds is not our doing. We did not do this! You have a mole somewhere that was able to get this kind of information. This is not something of which we approve. I know your reputation, so I wanted you to have this."

Schneid examined the names on the list, then folded it up and put it in his pocket. The next day, Schneid contacted and gave the paper to a trusted FBI agent.

Big Mac and Schneid agreed to have a series of follow-up meetings.

As Schneid got up to leave, Big Mac said, "Dr. Schneid, don't be late again."

It was an amazing hour. As shackled and defenseless as Big

Mac was, Schneid could feel and sense the awesome power be-hind this guy. He knew Big Mac could give an order and have him killed. Schneid witnessed his power when Big Mac questioned the Marshalls and the Lieutenant. Instead of them just telling him, "Go fuck yourself," they knew they had to respect him for the power that he possessed.

As he left the building, Schneid thought to himself, "That was fucking unbelievable!"

EMPTYING JACUZZIS
WITH A SPOON

*"Those who are serious in ridiculous matters
will be ridiculous in serious matters."*
- Cato the Elder

Frustrated with Jim's lack of progress kicking drugs, Dr. Schneid, a court-appointed substance abuse specialist, had a private conversation with the judge in his chambers.

"So, what are we going to do with him now?"

"Well, we've sent him to several different drug and alcohol rehab centers, and none of them have done a thing for him."

"So, what do you want to do?"

"Judge, let's extend the time for Jim at the center he's in now. Give me a court order to inspect the dozen or so clinics in Los Angeles County. I'll act as an ombudsman, evaluate their assets and practices, then report back to you."

Schneid pulled up to Jim's drug and alcohol rehabilitation center in Pasadena on a Tuesday. His rehab center visits were always unannounced. He would pop up like a mushroom after a good rain.

"So, Doctor Winston, how's Jim doing?"

"Jim who?"

"Jim Appel, one of your patients who's been here for more

than three weeks."

Heralded as the diamond of rehab facilities in the county, its head, and the only psychologist didn't know the name of a patient he was supposed to be rehabilitating.

Schneid gave up on the psychologist and headed to where all the counselors met weekly to decide which patients they were going to terminate, patients who weren't working the program. As the meeting progressed, he felt like he was Roman watching little emperors decide the fate of who was in the ring.

When Jim's name came up, Schneid spoke up. "Jim tells me that he has asked to meet with your psychologist three or four times. Is that true?"

"Yes, three times."

"Then why hasn't he seen the psychologist?"

Another counselor chimed in, "We keep turning Jim down to see just how eager he is to have an appointment. So we'll keep saying no, we're busy, and if he wants an appointment, he needs to say, "I really really want an appointment?"

Another counselor added, "We need to teach him how to be more humble."

"Ok, what if that doesn't work?

"Dr. Schneid, we're going to give him a tablespoon and have him empty the Jacuzzi with it. That'll teach him humility."

"So, your therapeutic interventions are to ignore his requests to see a psychologist to help him work things out and instead, have him empty a Jacuzzi with a tablespoon?

"Tell me what counseling qualifications do each of you have."

The leader replied, "I can speak for all of us. All of us are addicts who've been sober for at least a year. We know the game."

"Have any of you gone through academic training to become counselors?"

"No, Sir."

"Do any of you have college degrees?"

"No, Sir."

"Do you consult with your psychologist to develop treatment plans and make residency decisions?"

"No, Sir."

"So, as a group, you are coming up with patient treatment plans for Jim and other patients, and you're the ones deciding who will stay and who will leave here?"

"Yes, Sir."

"May I point out something about Jim?"

"Of course."

"He has low self-worth, so he's just not going to keep pestering you for an appointment, and if Jim gets any humbler, he's going to lose any self-esteem he has left. Psychologically speaking, it's a bad idea to humiliate someone like that by having him empty a Jacuzzi with a tablespoon."

Schneid parked in front of the rehab center on his list for the third time. He opened his briefcase and pulled out the center's activity chart and noted that it was vocational rehabilitation time. Patient vocational training sounded like excellent therapy to him. He walked through the gate and noticed patients picking weeds around the premises.

He found a counselor and asked, "What are those patients doing?"

"They're grooming the premises."

"Well, your chart says here that this is supposed to be vocational rehabilitation time and I'm looking at patients pulling weeds. Are they all studying horticulture or landscape architecture?"

"I don't know what you're talking about."

"Well, it says here from eleven to noon, vocational rehab and I'm looking at them all pulling weeds."

Schneid gave up on him and went into the kitchen area because they served lunch at noon. He saw one dietary civilian and maybe a dozen patients working in the kitchen getting lunch prepared. They also had patients building furniture to furnish the various cottages in which the patients lived.

"Is this part of vocational rehab?"

"No, this is their giving back to show their gratitude."

"Well, it seems to me that what they're doing is something short of slave labor, because you don't have to pay them to do your gardening or to do your food preparation."

"Wow, I would hardly consider it that."

"Then tell me how many paid employees you have here."

"You'll have to check with the administration."

The next day, Schneid visited a rehab facility in West L. A.

"I would like to see all of your patient charts."

Dr. Bologna, the licensed psychologist, fetched the charts and handed them to Schneid. He quickly examined all of their psych and behavioral notes.

"Doctor Bologna, for all of these patients, your group therapy notes only say that so-n-so attended group therapy this morning. Anyone reading these would get absolutely nothing about how patients participated in sessions and what was or wasn't their progress. I get nothing about any of the patients from your notes. Do you have other notes somewhere else?"

"No, and according to the law, that's all I'm required to do."

"Clinically speaking, these are useless."

This and other rehab facilities were using their patients as free labor to keep down expenses. Most of them had amateur counselors running the show and rarely had more than one staff psychologist on duty, no matter the patient load.

Their first year recidivism rate averaged 90% and the second year 80%, so there was always going to be an influx of patient inventory. The whole county had just two inspectors to ensure the facilities met their licensing standards, which included having only a single licensed psychologist, even if they had a hundred patients. It was apparent to Schneid that they had a lack of legal and medical incentive to cure these people.

Schneid did a background check of some of the non-profit center owners. They were driving expensive cars like Jaguars and Maseratis and had expensive homes and estates. This was not a bad racket for them as the centers were money making-machines with trimmed gardens and patients emptying Jacuzzis with a spoon, all paid for by Los Angeles County taxpayers.

THE YOUNG MANIPULATOR, INTO THE DARKNESS

"You're dating your mother?"

"Yeah, we sometimes go out on dates, and we give each other massages all the time too. So what? What's the big deal?"

"Well, you told me that yesterday that she came out of the shower, walked nude into your room, and asked you for a back-rub. Doesn't that seem unusual to you?"

"Dr. Schneid, Can we talk about something else."

"No. You brought up something important that has shaped your addictive narcissistic personality. Did you have sex with your mother yesterday?"

"Well, I was pretty wasted when she came in."

"Wasted on what, heroin?."

"No, just weed. She likes to get stoned with me."

"Are you still dealing pot?"

"If I tell you, will you report me to my probation officer?"

"Not for pot, according to the court, I'm only required to report heroin or coke usage."

"Ok, yeah, I'm dealing, and my mom likes to get loaded and get massaged, and maybe we messed around a little. So what?"

"That's borderline incestuous, and if you did more than mess around, then it's incest. Shane, your incestuous relationship with your mother, may have retarded your socialization skills and led to your self-destructive drug habits.

"Maybe, but it works for us and has for years."

"It does? Why did you break up with your girlfriend, Carla?"

"She thought my mom hated her and was trying to break us up."

"Was she?"

"Maybe. A couple of weeks ago, Carla and I were doing it in the bathtub and Mom walked in wearing a transparent negligee holding a couple of lit candles. She said it would be more romantic for us. Carla freaked out and left."

"Yeah, I can see why she would do that."

"Did it bother you that your mother intruded on Carla's intimate space with you?"

"Not really. At the time, I thought it was pretty cool, but Carla told her to fuck-off. We argued and then she split. I haven't seen her since. Good riddance to her. My mom's way hotter anyhow."

"Do you understand why most girlfriends might not like that kind of intrusion?"

"Kinda, but I don't give a shit. Girlfriends don't take care of me like my mom does, and she lets me do what I want with her."

"Shane, you use your good looks to get you what you want. You never have work, and you depend entirely on manipulating people to take care of you. How long do you think you can continue being a 'boy toy' to your mom and girls?"

"For as long as I feel like it."

Schneid came into his mother's room and gave his elderly mother a warm hug. He stepped aside and introduced Shane to her, then Shane put his hands on her shoulders and gently kissed her cheek.

After a few minutes of small talk, Shane excused himself to get a bite to eat from the cafeteria.

As soon as he left the room, she said, "Bill, a cold chill went through my whole body when he touched me. That young man is evil."

Schneid found that trying to assist Shane Graham to achieve some level of sobriety was virtually impossible. Shane repeatedly violated probation and wound up going to prison multiple times. He didn't mind so much because he quickly adjusted to prison life and became popular with fellow inmates. He used his good looks and intelligence to charm and manipulate both inmates and guards.

His dependencies on his mother and drugs were degrading him physically and mentally. He got to the point that he couldn't find any good veins. He got so desperate that he started injecting between his toes and into his neck's jugular vein. Finally, the only usable vein left was in his erect penis.

Schneid knew Shane's time was limited and wasn't surprised the day he got a call from Shane's sobbing mother, "He died this morning from an overdose while laying in the bathtub."

"Shadows speak your words. They change with the sun.
Sometimes there is no sun. The moon creates slurred speech.
Like a vampire, your soul can't stand the light of day.
Your heart seems so dead that I wonder if there are measurable beats.

You have an eternal life of your own punctuated by rhetoric new to this generation of the living.
Each person, each situation is subjected to the ageless you.
But to the naive, the uninformed-- it's all so new. So refreshing. So pleasant. So deadly.
But the trap must be laid ever-so-carefully lest anyone sense the real motive — the lust for a real life.
But, as vampires know, that is all but impossible. You can make it seem so very real. But your agenda is quite clear. It has been for all of time.
It is to take a life so that you might live. It is done without conscience. Without thought or remorse, as it must be. For you have your own will to 'live.'
You must, of course, have your allure as does the flame to the moth, a fine technique honed through the ages that allows you an almost instantaneous ability to sense blood coursing through a vein--or a wounded heart or hurting soul.
Your hands shake with the very excitement of your find. You are

trembling as you hold your unwitting prey.
Not quite yet. The timing has to be perfect. It must appear natural.
The victim must appear willing for your pure lust to be appeased.
How tantalizing it must be to hold total destruction in your power,
yet before you unleash it, you want to play with it a bit longer--as a
lion with its soon-to-be-killed."

-Bill Schneid

THE VISITOR

"The hot desert sand causes mirage ripples to distort the driver's vision.

The black roadway snakes its way seemingly 120 miles into nowhere from Los Angeles. Finally, the pathway ends in a patch of a desert canyon — the end of Highway 202, the Tehachapi Correctional Institution.

A welcome sign offers visitor parking. It's a bit of an illusion. All who come here are not visitors. The word visitor implies freedom to come, stay awhile, and leave at will.

For some, leave at will has no meaning.

A visitor registry book is open to signing in at this hostile hotel for the damned. A search of the visitor, i.d. checked and rechecked. The visitor drives up a tree-lined roadway. How seemingly benign. The real truth slams the visitor in the face. A fence, not to keep people from getting in but rather to keep people from getting out. A lacey pattern of barbed wire, signs warning of the fatal nature of touching the executioner's web. Concrete gray buildings with tassel-like outcroppings containing human beings, whose sole mission is to contain human beings. Signs scream out, "No warning shots."

The visitor waits, seeing a blue-denim cloth person in the distance, starting his long walk in a familiar gait. He is stopped in his mission. A reminder of the control as his permission for this moment of contact is checked. Not quite yet, he's searched.

Everyone must be protected.

The visitor speaks, and the highly charged emotions electrify the room, surely with more power than the fence itself. A momentary touch confirms the existing care and pain.

The visit ends as it began. He is searched. The visitor stands with him and his assigned officer. No one must move as the assigned officer calls out to the gun tower, "Raise the gun. Inmate to pass."

The blue-suited penguin starts walking away then glances back, whispering his shout, "Hey, thanks for caring," as he turns and walks back to his concrete igloo.

This was a good visit."

- Bill Schneid

Hunkered down in the boys' bathroom stall, Andy nervously loaded his father's Arminius 22 caliber long-rifle double-action revolver with an eight-shot capacity that he had taken from his father's locked gun cabinet. He took a deep breath, then opened the stall door and shot dead freshman Bryan Zucker in the back of the head as he stood in front of a urinal. Then he shot junior Trevor Edwards in the side of the neck.

Now on the floor, Trevor asked, "Why did you shoot me?"

"Shut up."

Everyone in the bathroom was scattering when Andy shot student-teacher Tim Estes and then security officer Peter Ruiz, who had stepped in to see who was setting off firecrackers.

Andy reloaded, walked out into the crowd in the hallway and started shooting, wounding more people and killing senior Randy Gordon. Six minutes and thirty bullets later, two students lay dead, and thirteen others were injured.

Cornered in the same bathroom by police, he called out, "It's only me," and threw down his weapon.

Andy, just fifteen years old and five foot four inches high, was a product of a broken marriage, sexual abuse, drugs, and alcohol abuse, school bullying, and finally, a dare to kill. After he started shooting, he blanked out and went into what criminologists call a dissociative fugue event. Ironically, those that he shot were none of the students who had taunted and bullied him.

Accompanied by a guard, Andy walked into the large gray room with ten gun-metal tables with metal seats attached and sat down across the table to face the balding criminologist. He was sixteen now and a few inches taller. He wore a faded blue denim shirt and work denim pants, standard Tehachapi State Prison inmate gear.

"Andy, my name is Dr. Bill Schneid. The Public Defender's Office hired me to check in on you. Since you're a minor in a maximum security adult facility, they are concerned about your general welfare."

"Are you a psychiatrist."

"No, I'm a criminologist."

"Criminologist? You mean you study criminal minds?"

"Yes, that's part of what I do. I also study how crime impacts society and recommend fixes. So, Andy, how are they treating you?"

"I'm okay. They keep me safe in solitary, and I have a cool roommate."

"Does that bother you, being in solitary?"

"Not really."

"Has anybody been bullying or taunting you?"

"No, not really."

"You got bullied a lot at school, right?"

"Yeah, a lot."

"Do you mind if I ask you something about that?"

"No."

"Did you choose the bathroom to be the place to start shooting because some older boys had repeatedly pushed you into the urinals and peed on you, not to mention stealing your money and stuff?"

"I guess I was hoping they would try it again. I hid in the stall for a while to wait and think things out. I wanted to create a big scene and get the police to kill me, but instead, I shot and killed innocent people. I didn't think it through. I lost control. I just wanted to get off this earth and out of my misery."

Schneid wanted to see Andy's cell. The guard spoke into his radio, "Clear the yard!" All the adult inmates went back to their housing units. Juvenile inmates are not permitted to be around adult prisoners. Once cleared, the guard, Andy, and Schneid walked across into his housing unit to see where he lived. It was a stark double-bunked concrete cell with a steel toilet and sink. A thick glass slit in the cinderblock wall allowed one to view the barren yard. Andy had a roommate. Another kid transplanted from Bakersfield had repeatedly stabbed his mother and now was in jail for attempted murder.

Andy got fifty years for his crimes. He will be eligible for parole in March 2025, when he is 39 years old.

A few miles from the prison, Schneid pulled his car over to the side of the road and wrote "The Visitor."

DAY TRIP TO SAN QUENTIN

"Drugs have taught an entire generation of American kids the metric system."
- P.J. O'Rourke

Jim Appel, at twenty-five years old, was smart and had a relatively benign carefree surfer type of personality. Everyone who knew him thought he was a nice guy. You would never believe that Jim was a tattooed addict. He didn't have a tattoo on him. For someone unemployed, he worked hard at picking up cans and bottles for recycling to have money. At the airport, Jim would pick up luggage carts and return them for a quarter each. When he was homeless, Schneid, the court-appointed substance abuse specialist assigned to his case, would ask Jim to call him every couple of days and he would. Back then, there were payphones all over the place.

Schneid would ask him, "How are you doing, Jim?"

"I'm doing alright. I just showered."

"Where did you shower?"

"At an apartment complex in Oakwood."

Jim was resourceful enough to know every apartment complex that had pools and showers outside and where they were. He would lay out on a chaise lounge to dry after showering.

"Did you eat?"

"Yeah, last night I had shrimp and some prime rib."

"Where in the world did you get that?"

Jim was also resourceful enough to know when every restaurant would throw out the food that not consumed for one reason or another, or a pizza place where somebody didn't pick up a pizza. It was amazing how well that lifestyle suited him.

A judge sentenced Jim to several drug rehab centers to no avail. Even when sentenced to jail, he quickly acclimated. Prison was like summer camp, just a novelty to him. Jimmy had their admiration because he could write and talk well. He wasn't your typical street thug, so he was no threat to anybody.

Jim got busted for possession while on probation once again. Schneid was running out of ideas of how to help him when Jim's sentencing judge called him into his chambers.

"What do we do with him this time?"

"Your honor, why don't we sentence him to a day at San Quentin?"

The judge thought it over. "I think that's a great idea. I'm going to order that."

"Ok, how are we going to get him up there?"

"You are going to get him up there."

"Are you serious?"

"I'll give you a court order and voucher. Get on a plane and fly him up to San Francisco with him where you'll rent a car and drive to San

Quentin. You make the arrangements with San Quentin. "

Schneid called the warden at San Quentin and told him he had a court order to sentence this guy to just one day at San Quentin.

The warden said, "I'll get back to you."

The next day, Schneid got a call from the California Attorney General's office. "We cannot have Superior Court judges all over California sentencing everybody to one day at San Quentin. There's a process, and logistically, it's just crazy."

"This is an exception. We've tried everything with this guy, and we're planning on this to scare the kid into getting straight before he ends up in a real jail like San Quentin for some capital crime. I would really appreciate it if you would make an exception this one time."

And they did.

So, they flew up, and Schneid got introduced to the head of the Special Enforcement Unit at San Quentin.

"Dr. Schneid, this is a 'no-hostage facility.' If inmates take either of you hostage, this jail won't pay a ransom or release somebody as a trade. That would be unfortunate, but that's the way it is."

They had been told not to wear Levi's and other specific types similar to the inmates' apparel. They didn't want to have any confusion as to who we were. So, they wore different clothes.

Their guard escort was someone everybody knew. He'd been working at San Quentin for a couple of decades. As they walked through the prison, Schneid sensed he was in the presence of evil. The population of the prison exuded it.

The inmates had to stay behind certain lines painted on the asphalt. They couldn't cross the line without being shot, but that didn't keep them from sauntering right up to the edge of the line to give sustained eye contact with Schneid and Jim. Bill could almost see their thoughts as they eviscerated him. It was as though they were trying to kill him mentally. As they moved through groups of inmates, they wouldn't move until they were inches away from them. They were showing him who they thought had the power.

As they walked around through the general population, the guard said, "Let me take you to Death Row."

The sign over that area said in an old English scroll, "You are now entering Death Row." For everyone's protection, they had locked down Death Row before they entered. All of the inmates were in their cells. It looked and sounded like a bad Fellini movie with inmates banging tin cups and grabbing at Schneid and Jim through the bars of their cells. They made a cacophony of screaming, yelling, and cursing. It was incredible. Schneid could barely stand the level of noise.

He thought, "I'd rather be in the jungles of Vietnam than here." There were hundreds of inmates on multiple tiers. All of them were "under the gun." The guards were fully armed, and signs said, "No warning shots."

This was serious business. The hundreds of people incarcerated there were all sentenced to death. So they didn't have anything to lose if they attacked and killed Schneid, Jim, another inmate or a guard. If they did, what was going to happen to them, sentence them to death twice? Being in that module made their hair stand on end.

As they walked out of Death Row, an elderly Black inmate grabbed hold of Jim's shirt. Now understand this had been prearranged and wouldn't normally happen. The inmate was a lifer, but a benign one who had been there for some forty years. He was the kind that a warden would allow for cleaning his house. He was a harmless man who had done something stupid as a teenager and wound up with a life sentence.

He grabbed hold of Jim and said, "You see that ledge over there?" There was an area below it where buses with new inmates arrived. "We always know when the buses are coming, so we all stand along that ledge. If you were one of them, I imagine I could have you for a carton of cigarettes, and you would be my bitch."

Jim said, "I wouldn't let that happen."

Schneid asked, "What would you do about it?"

"I would join the Aryan Brotherhood for protection."

The Black inmate laughed and said, "Join the AB's? What do you suppose it takes to be an AB?"

"I don't know, but I'm White."

The inmate replied, "Yes, but you have to be willing to kill somebody on command. So, White Boy, you willing to kill somebody on command?"

"Well, I don't know. I guess if I had to."

"Have you ever killed anybody?"

"No."

"You better start thinking about that and think about me

getting you for a carton of cigarettes because you're young and juicy. I might even have to fight for you if someone else wants you."

They returned to Los Angeles the next day. When back in court, the judge sentenced Jim to some additional probationary time. Sure enough, two weeks later, he violated probation again, and he was back in front of the judge.

Once again, everyone was disappointed. Schneid asked to speak to the judge in his chambers.

"I don't know what to do. I've tried everything. Judge, you've been kind enough to go along with every sentencing recommendation I've given, and now I'm plum out of ideas. This is very frustrating because I normally fix things."

The judge knew of Schneid's previous struggles with drug addiction, working as an undercover agent. He looked at Schneid and said, "Bill, don't get down on yourself. I see this as a winning situation for you."

"How do you figure?"

"Despite losing Jim to drugs, you're still sober. That's a win."

"I guess you're right."

Ultimately, two years later, Schneid got a call from Jim's mom, Susan, saying, "We just got home from the supermarket and Jim's dead. He had overdosed and collapsed dead in the hallway."

She asked Schneid to give his eulogy.

At Jim's memorial, Schneid addressed the gathering, "Ladies and gentlemen, I'm getting tired of doing this for young people. I'm running out of eulogies. Through the tears in my eyes, I see and feel your suffering. I am reminded that addiction doesn't just kill the addict. It kills the family and the caring people who tried to help!"

Jim was cremated and interned next to two other young men Schneid had tried to save, Shane and Mark. Each of their grave markers has a picture of each frozen in time of when they were young
and very much alive.

THE RELUCTANT HITMAN

*"Tricks and treachery are the practice of fools
that don't have brains enough to be honest."* - Benjamin Franklin

"Mark, who do you consider trustworthy in the narcotics unit of the Sheriff's Department? I want somebody experienced and trustworthy who knows how to get things done and will not blow my cover."

"Contact Inspector Doug Linn. He's been around for a while and knows the game."

While doing undercover work for the DEA, Schneid had come across several lower-echelon cocaine dealers in unincorporated areas who were too small for the DEA, which was going after bigger fish to fry. He wanted someone at the Los Angeles Sheriff's Department (LASD) to feed his information. So, he contacted Mark Bolter, who was an informant that he trusted. As the initial investigator, Schneid started to give some cases to Inspector Doug Linn at the LASD.

Whenever Schneid followed up with Linn as to what had happened to a particular case, Linn would say they were still working it. His response became so repetitive as to raise a red flag in Schneid's mind. He did some digging and discovered that the dealers he had turned in to Linn for prosecuting were still dealing. When he probed a little deeper, he found out that they were paying off Linn to allow them to do business as usual. In other words, he was extorting them.

Schneid looked into Linn's financial background and found out that he had a beautiful ranch up in Shasta County and that he was accumulating lots of expensive toys like boats and cars. So Schneid called Internal Affairs of the Sheriff's Department.

"Internal Affairs. Sam Escher speaking. Who's calling?"

"Special Agent Bill Schneid. Sam, you've got a bad apple in your department."

Schneid gave a full account of his suspicions to Officer Escher, who, instead of passing it up the line for a departmental investigation, called Doug Linn.

"Doug, you won't believe it, but we got a call from Special Agent Bill Schneid accusing you of extorting dope dealers. I can't believe you would do anything like that, so I thought you should have a heads up."

A worried Linn got hold of Mark Bolter and ordered him to put a hit on Schneid.

Schneid had always treated his informants with honest respect, so they were somewhat loyal to him. A few days later, Schneid got a phone call from Mark, who knew Schneid by the alias John Trevor.

"John, do you know a Doug Linn?"

"Yeah, I do. Last year, you referred me to him.

"Oh yeah, that's right. I forgot I had."

"Anyhow, you won't believe it, but Linn has put a contract out on you and ordered me to do the hit."

"What! That son-of-a-bitch needs to be brought down. Listen, would you be willing to talk to the Sheriff's Department that one of their drug enforcement investigators is extorting the dealers he was supposed to be busting?"

"If they can protect me from Linn, sure. I'll do it. He needs to be stopped. There's a whole lot of people who would like to see him go away."

"Mark, no worries. We'll get you into the witness protection program."

Schneid contacted a friend at LASD who he had known for

years and trusted with his life. Investigators put Mark in a hotel for several days to debrief him before putting him into the Witness Protection Program.

A formal high-level investigation followed which led to Linn's arrest, along with DEA Special Agent George Hoelker, who had partnered with Linn. They were charged with eleven counts, including extortion by threats of violence, conspiracy to possess and distribute cocaine and solicitation of a bribe. The extortion indictment alleged that Hoelker and Linn threatened a Jack Lang with physical violence to force Lang to sign a life insurance policy application" which "named defendant Hoelker as the beneficiary."

They were both convicted and sentenced to long terms in federal prison. The Internal Affairs officer got fired.

Schneid had a wonderful time testifying in federal court. As he gave testimony on the stand, he stared into Linn's eyes as he explained to the court how Linn had put out a contract hit on him. For him, that was just a really warm fuzzy feeling. It got even fuzzier when he heard the jury's guilty verdicts and then when the judge read out Linn and
Hoelker's sentences.

"YOU'RE JUST A MISDEMEANOR IN MY FELONY WORLD"

"Ok, Schneid, remind me again the cases you worked for me."

"You've got to be kidding. You don't remember?"

Schneid listed the five unpaid cases he had worked for FBI Senior Resident Special Agent Mark Hunter.

"Oh yeah, yeah."

"Mark, it's been almost six months, and I still haven't been paid for these cases."

"Oh yeah, I've got to get hold of the relevant agents and have them file their field reports to get you paid."

"Mark, you said that the last two times I spoke with you."

"Don't get testy with me, Schneid. You'll get paid when you get paid."

Schneid figured Hunter was bullshitting him, but he wasn't an official employee of the bureau, so he had no authority over any of agents, so it wasn't his place to call the supposed agents and tell them to file their relevant field reports so he could get paid.

Getting the runaround from Hunter had become more than just the proverbial pebble-in-the-shoe nuisance. Schneid needed to pay his bills. He decided he wasn't going to put up with it anymore, so he called the Office of the Inspector General for the DOJ, but he couldn't get through to anyone who could or would help him. Next, he called a friend at Quantico, then another enforcement friend and another. Nobody knew or could tell him anything, and what's more, they gave him no paths to resolution. He suspected they were purposely playing dumb.

Finally, he got through to some rookie agent at the L.A. Regional field office who sounded interested in what Schneid had to say.

"Agent Knupfer, I haven't gotten paid, and I don't know where else to go. Mark Hunter is the top dog of his satellite office, and I don't know who's above him.

"Dr. Schneid, I'm noting all of this."

"Agent Knupfer, thank you. All I want is to be paid for work done I've done for Hunter's satellite office. Like everyone else, I have bills to pay."

"I understand. Dr. Schneid, how long have you worked for the bureau?"

"About twenty years and I've never, I mean never, had a pay issue before. In fact, other bureau agents usually go out of their way to get me paid because I do good work for them. I have an exceptional service award from Director Mueller."

It couldn't have been ten minutes later, and his phone rang. It was Agent Mark.

"Bill, I understand you have a problem with me."

"Yes, Mark, I have a problem with you. It's called not getting paid by you."

"Well, I tell you what, Bill. I'll have all your money for you this Friday. We'll meet in the usual place in the parking lot of Alice's Restaurant."

They met in the parking lot where Mark and another agent slipped into Bill's back seat.

"Ok, Mark, over the phone, why did you sound so pissed off? I'm just trying to get paid what I'm owed."

"What do you mean, pissed off. Oh, I'm not pissed for anything you did, Bill. After all, you're just a misdemeanor in my felony world."

"You know, Mark, normally I would take that as an insult, but it's so ridiculously funny and incredibly insulting that I have to laugh at it. It's brilliant. I should put that on my tombstone, 'He was a misdemeanor in Mark's felony world.'"

In one short sentence, Schneid realized this agent did not consider him a valuable asset. During his long years working for the FBI, no agent had ever denigrated him like that. He had worked for dozens of special agents on hundreds of undercover assignments and never once had he encountered an unethical agent like Hunter.

Mark and another agent met Schneid in the usual parking lot. Mark pulled out a wad of bills and peeled off what the FBI owed Schneid.

"Ok, that does it, Schneid. We're through. We're done. You're paid up. Have a nice day."

The next morning, Schneid got a call from another bureau agent who wanted to work with him. "Bill, listen, it turns out I can't work with you."

"Why not?"

"I can't discuss it. I can't work with you. That's all I can say."

Schneid was baffled and got hold of a friend of his at another federal agency. "Tim, do me a favor. Call the bureau and say you're interested in employing me on a task force for your agency, and you want some background information."

A day later, Tim calls Schneid back. "You won't believe it. An agent named Hunter buried the hatchet in your back."

"You gotta be kidding. Mark's that petty. He knew he owed that money to me. He knew that I wasn't getting paid and he purposefully put me off for months. He can go fuck himself."

Hunter had written and filed a report that stated Schneid was difficult to work with, was hard to get information from and other bullshit. Because of the memo, Schneid never again worked for the bureau. He had been given the wrongful kiss of death with no way to appeal. In situations like that, senior agents could act with impunity.

Schneid wondered why the bureau had protected Hunter and been willing to sacrifice one of its top field operatives. There were a lot of Mormons in the FBI, including Hunter and the head of the L.A. office. Perhaps he had encountered another unethical Thin Blue Line.

Anyhow, that was the death blow for Schneid's FBI career. When somebody in the bureau wrote that kind of poison pen letter, you were done working for them. You didn't appeal it. You didn't do anything it. You were just gone.

But he was not gone from other federal law enforcement agencies. It may have been a loss for the bureau, but it was a significant gain for the other agencies he worked for because now he had more time for them.

APART FROM WORK STORIES

The following stories deal with recollections of Schneid's personal life, his dealings with wealthy people and high society, and his ability to outwit and manipulate people to achieve desired goals.

THE AIRHEADED HEIR

"Bad taste creates many more millionaires than good taste."
- Charles Bukowski

"Bill, you have to get up to my house right away."

"Why's that, Denny?"

"I have a deadline that I have to meet, and it's a security issue. I need you right away!"

"Ok, I'll be right over."

Schneid pulled into the broad circular driveway of Denny's East Gate Bel Air estate next to Jim Nabors' estate. Denny was standing next to his brand new custom-stretched Lincoln Continental.

"Bill, thanks for getting here so fast. Listen, I only have a couple of hours to make this decision."

He held up several samples of cloth and stared at Schneid. "I need your help with this."

"With what? Why are you holding up swatches of cloth?"

"Bill, I need to know whether or not you think the chauffeur's outfit should contrast or match the color of the car."

"You had me drive all the way up here for that?"

"Well, I only had a couple of hours to make a decision."

Later that year, Denny called Schneid's office. Global Projects, how may I be of assistance?"

"This is the QE2. This is the QE2. I have a call from a Mr. Denny Edwards for a Mr. Bill Schneid."

"This is Bill Schneid speaking."

"Please hold."

"Bill, it's me, Denny."

"Hey, Denny. How's goes it with your Indian Ocean-Mediterranean cruise?"

"Just great. Listen, we're docked in Port Said, Egypt for a few days, and I need for you to buy me a Rolls Royce Corniche in chestnut brown as soon as possible."

"I don't have that kind of money."

"That's not a problem. I'll move enough money into your account to cover it. I just heard that Rolls plans to raise their car prices ten percent next Monday. You've got five days to get it done. It should cost just over one hundred thousand dollars."

"Ok. I'll go down tomorrow once I see that the money is in my account."

"Bill, you're an angel. What would you like from Egypt? There's cool stuff here."

At that time, the rage was Egyptian scarabs and gold cartouches. "Denny, I would love to have an Egyptian scarab or a golden cartouche with my name engraved in hieroglyphics. You've seen them. Anyhow, either one would be nice."

A month later, Denny had Schneid stop by for lunch to give him his gift from Egypt. He handed Schneid a large and heavy box. Inside the box was a smaller one and then another. Finally, in the fourth box, he pulled out a heavy ten by twelve-inch scarab hand-carved out of ivory sitting on a solid malachite base.

Schneid was thinking, "Oh--my--god, this is ugly, big and very ugly."

"Oh my, Denny. You've really outdone yourself this time. I don't know how to thank you for this, this big beetle."

Such was life with Ogden (Denny) Edwards, an heir to Exxon Oil. He seemed to make money through osmosis. He had so much wealth that even when he made terrible business decisions, he could easily absorb the losses.

Denny had more money than brains or class befitting his position. His house was decorated exquisitely, not by him, but by expensive decorators. However, he had no idea what he had and didn't seem to care.

Denny, "This sofa is an original Austrian Biedermeier, and your malachite dining room table is a Louise XIV."

"Oh, they are? I haven't even sat on the sofa."

He knew nothing about his incredible furniture or ornaments, nor did he care.

Denny invited Schneid to bring a date to have Christmas dinner with him and a dozen friends at his mansion. They arrived and hors d'oeuvres, were served Gold Fish and mixed nuts along with cheap André champagne. Schneid quickly got bored with Denny's friends who were more interested in superficial small talk.

When it was time for dinner, two waiters seated them. A traditional five-piece place-settings adorned Denny's magnificent Louise IV table. His personal chef stood by to serve what Schneid hoped for and expected to be a fabulous haute cuisine dinner in the beautifully decorated millionaire's dining room.

They were seated with Denny at the head of the table. To his right sat Marlene Stevenson, Denny's beau. Denny reached into his pocket, pulled out a jeweler's box, opened it, and presented Marlene with a natural eighteen-carat canary diamond ring. It was big, and its yellow clarity was breathtakingly beautiful.

"Marlene, I know you love canaries, so I bought this yellow ring for you."

"Ok. Thank you. It's nice." Marlene looked at it for a brief moment, handed it to Schneid sitting next to her. She put it on the table next to her water glass and proceeded to ignore it for the rest of the dinner. She had no clue as to the rarity and value of the diamond, and what's more, Denny didn't seem to care that Marlene didn't to care.

Schneid leaned over and whispered to his date, "What airheads. That ring is worth well over a hundred thousand dollars. He could have

saved the money and made Marlene happy with a plastic bubblegum ring."

Then out came a large ham topped with cloves and canned pineapple circles with maraschino cherries poked in the middle of each circle. Schneid gasped as he scanned the spread of string beans with marshmallows, canned cranberries, canned yams, canned corn, mashed potatoes with gravy and Vons' rolls served with Blue Bonnet margarine. Schneid decided the chef must have snuck out and bought a pre-cooked Vons' dinner. However, it behooved him to be polite to his host, so he said, "Denny, you've outdone yourself with this spread and, oh boy, that looks like a mighty fine ham with all those pineapple circles and cherries."

"Golly, thanks, Bill. After all, Christmas is about sharing. I'm so blessed to have all of you here to enjoy this magnificent meal. Chef, once again, you have outdone yourself."

When the dessert arrived, Schneid almost choked on his cheap champagne. The chef walked into the elegant dining room with its Louis XIV table and set down a jello desert of an orange lobster on a green bed from a cheap mold similar to the ones his mom had in her kitchen. That's what multi-millionaire Denny's chef brought out of his to-die-for state-of-the-art gourmet kitchen. Schneid was astonished, but Denny was glowing with pride serving this gaudy lobster jello desert.

Schneid's date leaned to him and whispered, "This dinner makes your mother look like a gourmet cook."

Schneid whispered back, "Yes, and now I have definite proof that money can't buy class."

A TASTE OF CLASS

"Elegance never goes out of style."
- anonymous

Wallis Annenberg's waiter offered Schneid a tray of tasty Salmon Rillettes, and another refreshed his glass of Dom Perignon champagne. The conversation was lively around the beautifully set table. The eclectic group of fifteen brilliant but humble writers, directors, doctors, artists, and philanthropists reminded Schneid of his parents' intelligentsia dinner parties.

As the waiter set down a bowl of Lamb Navarin soup, he asked Schneid, "Sir, for your entree tonight, would you like the Steak Diane or Lobster Newburg in a Puff Pastry?"

"I'll have Von's ham with the cherries."

"I beg your pardon, Sir."

"Just kidding. I'll have the lobster."

Everything that came out of her chef's kitchen was delectable, including the Pear Tarte Tatin dessert. After dinner, they retired to her living room to sip Rémy Martin Louis XIII Cognac and chit-chat. Someone had just come from a South American trip and someone else from another part of the world. Everyone had a fascinating travel story.

Wallis Annenberg, daughter of the Walter Annenberg, was extremely wealthy and a class act. She wasn't snobbish in the least and the way she handled her wealth paralleled her erudite personality.

Schneid met Wallis at the Beverly Hills Medical Center when he was coming off of drugs from his undercover work. Initially, he had no clue as to who she was other than she was a nice lady named Wallis. She was Schneid addiction counselor. One day, she said to him, "Bill, you need to get your parents to go with you to Al-Anon meetings."

So, he called his parents. "Mom, you and dad need to go to a local Al-Anon meeting to help me with my recovery."

She paused, then snapped back, "Son, you know those aren't our kind of people."

Schneid told Wallis, and she replied, "Well, let me talk to her."

She called and let his mother have it. "Mrs. Schneid, this is Wallis Annenberg. Perhaps you know of my family. Mrs. Schneid, I can assure you that the Al-Anon people in my chapter are your kind of people, just as they are my kind of people."

Schneid was in the room when she spoke. His mouth gaped open when he heard who she was. Until then, he didn't even know Wallis' last name, and here she is, a social A-lister, telling his snooty mother, "Mrs. Schneid we are your kind of people."

Wallis lived in Beverly Hills. At the time, her father was the U.S. Ambassador to the United Kingdom during the Nixon administration, so when they came to dine at her house, Secret Service always asked the guests a lot of questions. Her house was exquisite with impeccable taste and, unlike Denny Edwards, she knew everything about all that was in her home.

Schneid thought, "Both of them had grown up surrounded by wealth, but the difference between them was in large part because one of them had grown up surrounded by intellects and the other had not."

Wallis was a class act, and Denny would always be Denny.

THERE ARE JAPANESE
IN MY CORN

"You cannot invade the mainland United States.
Behind every ear of corn is an American with a rifle."
- Admiral Isoroku Yamamoto's gardener,
- Choki Watanabe

Schneid had an empty lot next to his well-manicured foot-hills' estate. He decided to plant corn on it. They planted an area ten by twelve feet in size with eight or nine rows. When the corn started to produce ears, he noticed a bug on a leaf.

He took it down to his local Ace Hardware and asked, "What the hell is this bug?"

"I don't know. It's a beetle that I've never seen before."

"Well shit, I don't want a corn infection destroying my corn crop."

He went home and called up the U.S. Dept. of Agriculture in Riverside. "I have this corn, and I have this bug on it, and I don't know what the bug is."

"Well, Sir, we only service farmers."

"I'm a farmer."

"Oh, well then we'll send out an agricultural expert out to your farm."

"Ok."

The next day, an Ag official pulled up in a big official Ag vehicle.

"Hi, I'm Dwight Carlisle with the Department of Agriculture. Do I have the right address?"

"Yes, Sir."

"Really? Well, I'm looking for a farm."

"I've got a farm."

"Did you call us regarding some insect infesting your corn?"

"Yes, Sir, I did."

"Where's the farm."

"Right over there."

Schneid walked the inspector over to the corn patch.

"That's no farm. That's a corn patch. It's is only about ten by twelve feet."

"Well, I think of it as a farm. Nobody asked me how big it is or how big it had to be called a farm."

"Have you ever lived or been on a real farm before?"

"No, I grew up in West Los Angeles, and I've never had the pleasure of visiting a 'real' farm."

The expert sighed and said, "Listen, we don't come out just for some little family plot."

"I didn't know that."

"Well, I'm here, so let me take a look at your bug."

Schneid took him inside his house and showed him the bug.

"Oh my, what you have here is a Popillia japonica Newman beetle, commonly known as a Japanese Beetle. This is not good. They're very destructive, and they're not supposed to be in inland Southern California."

"Japanese? How the hell did it get here all the way from Japan?"

"We think it first came into the U.S. in the early 20th century through New York City in shipments of iris bulbs from Japan. It's a very destructive bug, especially to grapes, grapes, tomatoes, squash, and corn, to name a few. Lately, Ag inspectors have found a few in airports along the West Coast, including L. A.'s international airport but this is the first time we've seen them so far inland."

"How do you kill them?"

"Well, besides picking them off by hand, you can use a dish-soap based watery mixture to spray all over the leaves."

"That's it?"

"That's all we got at the moment. We're working on biological controls, but they're not yet available commercially. I've got some bad news for you."

"Besides the beetle, what?"

"We're going to have to quarantine your patch."

"Can we eat the corn?"

"You can but don't take any off the property. We'll be setting up traps and coming by once a week to inspect them until the corn is harvested and stalks removed."

"So, are you glad I called you guys about my farm's bug?"

"Yes, but please stop calling it a farm. It's a patch."

DECEIVING KENYA'S PRESIDENT MOI

"I call on all ministers, assistant ministers and every other person to sing like parrots. You ought to sing the song I sing. If I put a full stop, you should put a full stop. This is how the country will move forward..."
- President Daniel Moi

"Geoffrey, I would like visas for myself and two companions."

"Dr. Schneid, how long will you be staying in Kenya?"

"Several weeks."

"May I ask what you are planning to do in my fine country?"

"After arriving in Nairobi, we hope to go on a first-class photo safari."

"I see and in what hotel will you be staying while in Nairobi?"

"I have yet to book a hotel there. However, I prefer five-star hotels wherever I travel."

"Doctor, I happen to know the General Sales Manager of the Intercontinental. He is my cousin."

"Well, that's very convenient."

"Yes, would you like me to have him contact you. He would be able to arrange your every hotel need, and if you haven't already booked a photo safari, I also have a friend who could arrange an exceptional trip for you, one where you will not be treated like a herded tourist."

"That sounds wonderful."

"One more thing. Dr. Schneid, since you are such a very wealthy man, have you thought of making any donations to my poor but proud country?"

Schneid's eyes glazed over as he realized the consulate official was now trying to shake him down because he thought Schneid was super-wealthy. He thought, "He's going to get kickbacks from everything Geoffrey arranges through his family and friends, so why is he also asking me about making a donation?"

Always quick on his feet, Schneid replied, "You know, I was going to give a sizable donation to the Flying Doctors who do an incredible job of giving medical aid to your more remote tribes. They have amazing teams. Why, just yesterday, I called them up at their headquarters in Nairobi and asked them about what equipment they most needed. They mentioned blood pressure meters, stethoscopes, and several other basic necessities for diagnostic purposes. I told them that I would donate all that they needed."

"Dr. Schneid, have you thought of donating anything to our government?"

"Who's your president?"

"Daniel Moi."

"Well, I tell you what, besides my donation to the Flying Doctors, I will give $100,000 to President Moi's favorite charity?"

"Oh my, Dr. Schneid, that would be fantastic! With your permission, I will contact the President's office. Would you mind if I make your hotel and safari arrangements?"

"Well, of course, by all means. That is very generous of you. Thank you, Geoffrey."

Schneid had no intention of donating so much money to the President's charity because he knew it would all wind up in his uncharitable pocket. A skilled deceiver from so many years of working undercover, Schneid was definitely on his game that day. With zero trepidation, he looked forward to seeing how his clever ruse might play out. He would not be disappointed.

When Schneid and two traveling companions arrived at Jomo Kenyatta International Airport, a limousine picked them up and took them to the five-star Intercontinental Hotel in downtown Nairobi. Upon arriving at the hotel, Geoffrey's cousin, Moses Chemosin, greeted them with a huge smile and firm handshake. He took them up to a beautiful suite overlooking the city.

"Dr. Schneid, I will be at your disposal for anything and everything you and your companions may desire."

"Wonderful. We look forward to exploring your famous country."

They were in the room barely fifteen minutes when the phone rang.

"Dr. Schneid, I am James Adamu, First Secretary to President Moi. President Moi sends his greetings. He is most grateful for your generous charitable offer and would like to meet you. In the meantime, I will ensure that suitable arrangements are made for you on behalf of President Moi."

So far, Schneid's contrivance of generosity had worked its charm.

"Why, that would be wonderful."

"When are you planning to go on safari?"

"I'm not sure. Geoffrey Mwangi at your Los Angeles consulate told us a special photo safari would be arranged after we arrived in Nairobi?"

"Good, because a special safari is being arranged as we speak. Once the arrangements are confirmed, I will contact you."

The next morning, Schneid got a call from the front desk saying that the head of the Kenyan Postal Service was at the hotel and wanted to have breakfast with him.

"I'll be down in ten minutes."

Schneid knew immediately from his government intelligence work that this man was about as likely to be the head of their postal service as Schneid was a giraffe herder. He was obviously a high official from their intelligence service.

After exchanging greetings and pleasantries, the official queried Schneid seeking personal information. Schneid could easily tell by the nature of his questions that this supposed postal guy was vetting Schneid to get an idea of who and what he was all about to protect President Moi. The breakfast was a very cordial one, and the official left with the impression that Dr. Schneid was a wealthy and generous doctor.

Tired from their long Los Angeles to Nairobi journey, Schneid and his friends were lounging at the pool when a waiter brought a phone to Schneid.

"Dr. Schneid, this is James Adamu. I am pleased to inform you that Mr. Chemosin has completed your safari arrangements.

"Well, that's just wonderful."

"If it is convenient for you, the President's personal aide and safari guide, Daniel Omondi, will come to meet you in your hotel lobby today at 2:00 p.m."

"That would be fine."

Daniel arrived early and immediately impressed them with his kindness and articulate nature. Schneid thought Daniel's English was better than his own, and this tall powerful-looking Black man knew his stuff.

As they talked, Schneid mentioned that he had seen some beautiful decorative wood carvings of Kenyan animals in the hotel gift shop that were selling between $30 and $40.

"Dr. Schneid, would you like me to take you to where they are carved."

He took them to a warehouse in a Nairobi neighborhood where Kenyan artisans sat on the floor carving wooden animals, many identical to the ones in the hotel.

Schneid picked up a set of three-foot-high giraffes on which one carver was working. Schneid asked the price. Daniel spoke to the carver in the Kikamba language. The man looked up at Schneid and then spoke something to Daniel.

"Bwana, Mr. Mwendwa is pleased to meet you and would like you to know that he is a proud Kamba tribal member from near Mt. Kenya and that his giraffes and other animals are made from the wood of the wild olive tree. He is honored that you so admire his work and is offering you all three for $5."

"Please tell Mr. Mwendwa that I accept his price, that I am equally
honored to meet him and that I look forward to displaying his fine work
in my Los Angeles home."

At those prices, Schneid thought, "Wow, I could buy all the carvings in this warehouse and make a fortune selling them in California."

Before sunrise the next day, they took off northward into the wilderness with Daniel driving a safari-outfitted Land Rover. Most of the time, they traveled off-road through woodlands, croplands, and vast stretches of bushland. Without any road signs or significant landscape features, Schneid thought, "How the hell does this guy know where he's going?"

It was hot and dry when Daniel pulled up to a place called Buffalo Springs with a large natural spring-fed pool for them to freshen up and cool off. They luxuriated in the clear, cool spring waters before having cut fruits and drinks set out by Daniel under a large acacia tree. Schneid pulled out a little guide book and looked up Buffalo Springs.

"Caution, Buffalo Springs is known to have Cryptosporidium and Giardia parasites. People with open sores should not go in it."

Cryptosporidium

Giardia

After driving for miles through woodlands and then forest-lands full of wild animals, they stopped at the five-star Mount Kenya Safari Club on the slopes of Mt. Kenya smack on the equator. In 1959, actor William Holden and two partners had established the hotel club. They walked into the hotel and Daniel said something in Swahili to the concierge. The concierge quickly escorted them to the members-only area in the back where they enjoyed a delicious lunch.

From there, they headed westward and came upon a herd of maybe a dozen elephants. Daniel stopped, and they stepped out of the Land Rover for a better look. The bull elephant that was in charge of the herd turned and looked at them. He quickly decided they were a threat. He bellowed and charged at them. They jumped back into the Land Rover and just barely escaped his charge.

They spent their first night at a comfortable safari camp with tents of wooden floors and small "facility" tents behind each.

Daniel cautioned them to not go outside of the tent after dark. They did as they were told.

At dawn the next morning, Daniel came up to their tent and awakened them. "Bwana, it's time to get dressed. Breakfast will be served in twenty minutes. I hope you slept well."

Schneid called out, "We slept like logs and didn't hear a thing."

He got up and opened his tent flap to get some air. Right in front of the tent was a massive pile of poop from some big creature.

At breakfast, he asked, "Daniel what kind of creature left that huge

pile of shit in front of our tent?

With a big smile, Daniel declared, "Oh, it was probably that bull elephant who charged us."

After breakfast, they headed toward the Massai Mara Plains. Along the way, Daniel suddenly stopped the Land Rover, pointed and quietly said, "Bwana, look at that."

Schneid didn't see a thing other than a large acacia tree.

"Daniel, what do you see?"

"A leopard in the tree. He's resting on the large lower branch on the left side."

Schneid was amazed by Daniel's eyesight.

"I don't see any leopard."

He put on his 500mm camera lens and looked. "Ok, now I see it. Wow, look at those glowing green eyes."

On they drove until they pulled up to a safari camp next to a lake. Schneid asked Daniel if they could go out on the lake for some sunset photos.

"Dr. Schneid, on-the-lake tours are not normally permitted at this hour, and the manager has just turned away that group of tourists. However, I'll see what I can do."

Daniel spoke a few words in Swahili to the manager.

"Dr. Schneid, the manager says he would be honored to take us onto the lake."

The group of tourists stood watching with their mouths

open, Schneid's little group went out onto the lake. He captured breathtaking photos that are still on his wall at home.

The next day was full of wonderful sights. Daniel took them places few tourists ever got to see. That night, they stayed at the famous Treetops Lodge. The multistoried wooden hotel on stilts sits next to a natural waterhole and adjacent salt lick close to one side of the hotel. Animals come from miles to lick the salt and drink from the waterhole. Below the lodge and close to the salt lick is a concrete bunker with a narrow two-foot wide opening, not wide enough for an animal to get through, but wide enough for people to safely watch animals close up. At night, floodlights come on and whenever animals come up to the salt lick a bell system chimes in all of the guest rooms. One ring would go off if it were some interesting animal, two rings if it was really interesting and three rings if it was some animal or event rarely seen.

When Schneid heard three rings at dusk, he scrambled down to the bunker with all of his expensive camera gear. Daniel was already in the bunker, watching a critically endangered black rhino had come into view about a football field away.

"Bwana, a black rhino has not been seen in this sector for years."

Schneid screwed on his 500 mm lens and snapped a couple of photos. The rhino approached at a steady pace forcing Schneid to change to smaller lenses rapidly. Finally, the rhino got so close even his 50 mm lens was not wide enough to capture the whole animal. He
was awestruck as the rhino casually gazed at him.

He quietly murmured, "Thank you, President Moi, for this incredible gift."

The next day, Daniel took them to meet the Samburu people, a sub-tribe of the greater Maasai tribe. Schneid had a Polaroid camera that he used to check lighting conditions and composition before shooting with 35 mm Kodak films. Speaking their Swahili dialect, Daniel introduced the Americans to the tribe.

"My God, Daniel, how many languages and dialects do you

speak?"

"I don't know, Doctor, but I think as many as there are in Kenya, plus English, German and French."

Daniel told the tribal leaders that the Americans were special guests of the president. So the whole tribe starts singing and dancing for them as Schneid took pictures and taped them with a portable tape recorder. Before he started using his single-lens reflex camera, he took some Polaroids. When the tribe stopped dancing, he did a soundcheck. When the tribe heard themselves on the tape, they told Daniel they thought Schneid's capturing of their voices might be a gift from the gods.

When Schneid showed them the Polaroids, they went completely nuts and told Daniel that now they were convinced that the gods had sent to them Schneid, who obviously possessed supernatural qualities. They had never seen pictures of themselves and had never heard their voices. Not only had Schneid captured their voices, but he had also captured their souls in his images.

"Dr. Schneid, would you be so kind as to give them the Polaroids? It would be an incredible gift for them."

"Of course," and Schneid did so. The Samburu were so pleased they started dancing and singing again.

As Schneid watched them dance and jump high into the air, he asked, "Daniel, why do the women wear so many beads around their necks and why do some have more than others?"

With a big smile, Daniel responded, "Dr. Schneid, the louder they are while having sex, the more beads they get. Look, the ones who are singing the loudest have the most beads?"

"You're shittin' me, aren't you?"

"No Bwana."

"So, the tall, beautiful lady over there with the most beads must be the loudest in the tribe."

"Ha-ha, yes, Bwana."

Two tribal leaders came up and offered Schneid a cup of red liquid.

"Daniel, what is this?"

"It is an honored gift from them to you."

"Great, what is it?"

"They just bled one of their prized cattle. That is fresh blood from their best cow."

Schneid had never drunk fresh blood, nor had he ever imagined doing so. Scores of tribesmen, many of which had spears, watched his every move and waited for him to sip their honored gift.

He thought, "Shit, I'll gag and throw up if I drink this."

Daniel whispered to him, "I would drink the blood before it clots."

Well, that was the last thing Schneid needed to hear.

Trapped, he thought, "Well if my mother can eat calf brains and other sweetbreads, which I detest, and my Mexican friends can eat menudo, which is cow's stomach lining, how bad can a sip of blood be? I know the taste of blood from licking cuts on my fingers, and it wasn't so bad. So go for it."

From this wooden cup, he carefully took and swallowed a sip of the warm blood while pretending it was red wine. He didn't throw up, and he had saved face. Yes, he was still a god to them. Fortunately, he wasn't obligated to drink any more of it. Politely, he put his hand up and said to the tribe in his American English, "I'm full, I can't handle another drop of your cow's delicious blood. Your hospitality so very honors me. You are indeed a great tribe!"

With a huge smile on his face, Daniel translated what he said. The whole tribe cheered wildly. To this day, they probably speak of the time when the prominent White American bestowed magic and honor upon them.

On their last day on safari, they drove through the bush on the way to some massive waterfalls when suddenly a baby Wildebeest bounded in front of the Land Rover closely followed by a lioness. They screeched to a halt and watched the lioness bring down the little Wildebeest with her jaws wrapped around its throat, suffocated it.

Not far from the falls, Daniel brought them to a regular safari stop on the edge of a river that offered safe and incredible views of thousands of migrating Wildebeest crossing the crocodile-infested river in front of them. Other safari groups were already there standing along an embankment too high and steep for the crocs to get up, although a few of the crocs kept trying.

One of the tour guides was throwing pieces of chicken toward a little sandy area just below from where the tourists were standing. The crocs grabbed the chicken parts right out of the air. A woman at the very edge of the embankment snapped pictures with her expensive camera without the camera strap around her neck. The camera slipped out of her hand and down into the mouth of one of the crocs. Schneid could hear the motor drive going off inside the croc's jaws.

The woman screamed, "Oh my God. I've lost my camera!"

Finding it amusing, Schneid yelled back to her, "Yes, you have, but can you imagine the pictures it's getting!"

When they got back to Nairobi, the Director of Sales was waiting in the lobby of the Intercontinental Hotel. "Dr. Schneid, Secretary James Adamu has left several messages asking for you to call him. Here is his number."

"Secretary Adamu, this is Dr. Schneid."

"Ah, Dr. Schneid. How good it is to hear from you. How was

your safari?"

"Incredible, just magnificent. Moses booked us a fabulous safari, and Daniel was a superb guide."

"The President will be very pleased to hear that. He would like to have tea with you tomorrow at 10:00 a.m. If that is agreeable with you, we will send a driver."

Schneid figured that by now, the postal guy would have debriefed Moi and all was well enough for the President to meet with him. He knew what the President looked like because in every building in Kenya hung a picture of him. You had to be blind not to know.

Schneid was picked up and driven to the State House, the official residence of the President. He was escorted down a long hallway and into a well-furnished Colonial-style office. After a few minutes, President Moi walked in.

"Greetings my friend from California. Please sit down and tell me all about your magnificent safari. How did my beloved Daniel treat you?" They engaged in small talk, and Schneid asked what he did before he was elected President.

"I was a high school teacher before I became the Minister of Education."

"Interesting. Mr. President, tell me about one of the remarkable things you've accomplished since becoming President."

"Well, let me see. That is a difficult question. There are so many. Hmm. I have one of which I am very proud. I initiated an Executive Order banning the importation of chicken eggs."

"Oh, I didn't know Kenya had a problem with an overabundance of commercial eggs here."

"Oh, no, we don't. As a matter of fact, we have a scarcity of eggs. I just thought it was a remarkable thing to do."

"Yes, Mr. President, indeed you did something truly remarkable."

"Mpaka baadaye." The following day, Schneid said goodbye to Moses and the hotel staff that had made their Kenyan vacation one of the best he had ever had.

Every so often, Schneid would get a call from Kenyan Consulate officials inquiring about when they might receive his donation. "It's being arranged," was his usual answer. After a year, the Kenyan Consulate gave up and finally stopped calling."

For Moses, Schneid bought a fully-paid holiday on the remote island of Lamu, Kenya. He stayed in a well-appointed manor built by the Rothschild's of France. When his scam was found out, Schneid figured Moses would need a good place to hide in case Presidente Moi came looking for him.

And yes, the Flying Doctors did receive a generous donation of blood pressure meters, stethoscopes, and other needed medical equipment from a Dr. Schneid in California, who understood their needs.

AS A LICENSED PRIVATE INVESTIGATOR & SECURITY EXPERT

Before incurring significant wounds and injuries while on duty, plus a rare and debilitating spinal infection, Schneid took on private security details. When he could no longer physically work in the field, he established elite private investigation firms that protected Fortune 500 companies and uncovered the United States most massive medical fraud scheme.

As the lead investigator and owner of Global Projects and then Apex Strategic Investigations Group, he still communicates with operatives all over the world who provide him with strategic global insights and fascinating tidbits of information, such as what occurred on the USS Carl Vinson the night Osama bin Laden's body dropped into the North Arabian Sea.

RESCUING HOWARD HUGHES

"I'm not a paranoid deranged millionaire.
Goddamit, I'm a billionaire."
- Howard Hughes

A flat monotone voice on the other end of the overseas line spoke, "Mr. Smith, your subject has arrived in Tel Aviv and has met with your target."

"Great, continue to follow him."

The voice dropped the other shoe and said, "Do you ever want him to be seen again?"

"Well, yes. Don't do anything crazy."

"Ok, we will continue to report to you where he goes and who he meets with."

Starting in 1967, Howard Hughes Jr. had purchased several Las Vegas hotel-casinos and real estate on and off the Strip. The Mob was pissed off because Hughes did not allow illegal skimming in his casino operations. So in 1969, they came up with an elaborate plot to get those hotels back so they could resume their profitable skimming operations.

The plot revolved around finding a relatively unknown author living outside of the U.S. They would have the author create a fake Howard Hughes Jr. autobiography that made him out to be pathologically eccentric and crazy. The Nevada Gaming

Commission, who the Mob could leverage, would then order Hughes to appear for a fitness hearing. Because Hughes was such a recluse, they figured he wouldn't appear, which would result in the forfeiture of his licenses. They also thought he would never draw attention to himself by challenging such an autobiography or file a lawsuit for libel.

The plot was dreamed up and coordinated by former Jewish New York gangster and Mob bagman Meyer Lansky. Lansky had been and was the brains behind mob gambling operations in Cuba, London, the Bahamas, Florida, New Orleans, and Las Vegas.

Lansky met with Jewish Robert Maheu, who was Hughes' Chief Executive of Nevada operations. He was also an ex-FBI agent and an active CIA contract operative. Lansky wanted to see if he could get Maheu on board with the plot. Maheu agreed to assist and got hold of a Mob ally who might know of an unethical author. Hank Greenspun, the Jewish owner of the *Las Vegas Sun* newspaper, joined the effort.

Greenspun knew of a fairly nondescript writer by the name of Clifford Irving, who was living in Palma de Mallorca, Spain. Irving, seeing a chance to make some big money, teamed up with another author to produce a damning authorized autobiography. Their autobiography even included fake memoirs that were supposedly written by Hughes.

However, Hughes had allies within the CIA after assisting it with the raising of a sunken two thousand ton Soviet nuclear submarine from an ocean depth of seventeen thousand feet. Besides his security team, the CIA backed International Intelligence, Inc., known as Intertel, protected Hughes. It was the security arm of Resorts International and for decades served as a significant shadow link between the underworld and legal figures and entities. Former upper echelon department heads of U.S. law enforcement and intelligence agencies ran Intertel.

When Intertel got wind of the plot, they formed an international task force that included Schneid. The team built a full profile of the Mob plot to neutralize it.

Their first assignment was to monitor any Robert Maheu meetings with Meyer Lansky in Israel. In 1970, Lansky, a Jew, fled to Israel to escape a federal grand jury indictment for tax evasion. He thought that Israel's Law of Return would prevent the U.S. from extraditing him. By being in the Mediterranean, Lansky was able to monitor Clifford Irving's progress.

Schneid used their Israeli Massad contacts. Maheu didn't know that they knew that he was double-crossing Hughes, and was in the pocket of the Mob. He wasn't doing anything illegal, just totally unethical. He was merely doing it for money.

The Mossad addressed Schneid by the code name Mr. Smith.

They assured Mr. Smith that they would be willing and able to take on the responsibility of keeping tabs on Mr. Maheu.

"Mr. Smith, we will know when your target arrives. We know everybody who comes in and out of Ben Gurion Airport."

"How do you know so much?"

"We have our ways, and we work long into the dark of night."

The Mossad called Mr. Smith when Maheu left Israel. He was picked up for questioning during a meeting with Greenspun in Las Vegas.

Under pressure from the U.S. government and because of his past criminal record, the Israeli government deported Lansky back to the U.S. The authorities arrested Lansky when he landed at Miami Airport.

Hughes' team briefed him on the Mob's efforts to get him out of the Las Vegas hotel gaming industry. Hughes then exposed Clifford as a fraud through a partially televised telephone conference with journalists. The elaborate plot of the Mob and Clifford Irving to rid Hughes of his Vegas holdings soon vanished into thin air. The disgraced Irving subsequently went to jail and eventually disappeared into relative obscurity.

With the help of Schneid's Mossad connections, Hughes, who had spent over three hundred million dollars on his Vegas properties, was able to retain ownership of the hotel-casinos. The golden age of Mob rule in Vegas was over. The Mob never regained their former imminence.

AN INCH FROM BEING SHOT, A WORD FROM BEING DROPPED

"God did not create gays and lesbians so He could have something to hate!"
- Troy Perry

"Joe, I've got sights on a rifle barrel sticking out of a drop ceiling access panel in the crown molding, center back. It's aimed at Troy. Get up there asap."

"Bill, have no visual from my position. On my way. Standby."

Troy Perry, the founder of a church that focused on ministry to the lesbian, gay, bisexual, and transgender communities, was addressing a large congregation in Los Angeles Ambassador Hotel's Grand Ballroom.

Troy's voice rang out over the crowd, "If you love the Lord today, would you say, 'Amen'?"

"Amen!"

"I spoke to God and said, 'God, you can't love me because I'm a practicing homosexual.' And all at once God spoke to me and said, 'Troy, don't tell me what I can and can't do. I love you. You are my son. I don't have step-sons and step-daughters. I love y'all, amen!"

"Amen!

Troy had received many death threats from homophobes and exceptionally dumb idiots. He needed protection, so Schneid and Joe Donovan were hired to be his executive protection detail.

Joe DuPont stood in the back right corner of the ballroom. Schneid was scanning the audience from his four o'clock position behind Troy when he noticed movement above the crowd. A rifle appeared from a foot-square opening in the crown molding in the back of the room. He thought, "That could be an access panel from the catwalk space above the drop ceiling."

Schneid had told Troy that if he thought he was in danger, he would call out the word "drop" and Troy was expected to hit the ground, or in this case, the stage. They had practiced a couple of times before and laughed about it. Now, it might be for real.

Troy was already in full oratory stride, and his audience was enthralled, but Schneid was on DEFCON 1 waiting for Joe to get to the rifleman. His mind raced in fast forward trying to decide what to do.

"Oh, shit. RFK was assassinated here ten years ago, and there was this lady in a polka dot dress and...and...

"Keep focused, Bill.

"Ok, can I neutralize that shooter from here? No, but I could throw his aim off, but if I tell Troy to drop now in front of all these people, they will panic."

"Bill, I'm almost there!"

"We're out of time. I need to drop Troy now. There's no way I'm going to let this guy take out Troy on my watch."

Schneid opened his mouth to call out when he heard Joe's voice on the radio, "Target neutralized! Repeat, Target is down and secured."

"Good work, Joe."

"Hey, Bill, that rifle you saw is a handheld telescope. Our telescope-assassin is a janitor here. He says he goes up there all the time to watch the performances."

When the detail finished, Joe and Schneid went back to

Schneid's house to unwind in his hot tub. For both of them, especially Schneid, it had been a stressful day.

Joe thought the whole incident was hilarious. "Bill, I hit that janitor with a flying tackle. You should have seen his face. You had me believing his telescope was a rifle."

"Look, Joe, from over fifty feet away in that dimly lit ballroom, anybody, even you, would have thought that telescope was a rifle barrel.

"You know, that guy came within an inch of being shot by you or me and Troy came within a word of being dropped.

"Hello, this is Yellow Cab. What's your location and destination?"

"This is Bill Schneid. I'm the head of a security detail at the Lesbian and Gay Rights march. It has started to rain, and I need twenty-three cabs asap at the corner of 4th and Pennsylvania."

"Are you kidding me? You need how many cabs right now?"

"I'm serious. Can you get me that many cabs?"

"I can do maybe six or seven. That's all. We're pretty busy right now moving people to the march."

Schneid hung up and called the Secret Service Center. "Bill Schneid, security detail for Troy Perry here. I need to get me twenty-three cabs asap."

"Ok, where do you want them?"

Twenty-three cabs arrived within fifteen minutes to move the Perry entourage to the Washington Monument where a stage had been set up for the event speakers.

"Joe, this is bat-shit crazy. How the fuck are we going to keep Troy safe on the Mall tonight in front of over a hundred-thousand people holding candles?"

"You're right. This is a fucking nightmare. Look at all those flashes going off. Even with the Park Police and Secret Service helping, we need about a thousand more security personnel.

"Joe, we'd have a snowball's chance in hell trying to catch any assassin or assassins."

"Yeah, and it would be nice to have bullet-proof glass in front and to the sides of the podium."

Days before the march, Schneid, and Joe had met with security officials from the Park Police, D.C. Police Department and Secret Service.

"Hey Schneid, how do you feel about putting your life on the line for these fags?"

"Agent Kilpatrick, Troy pays well."

Troy got through his speech to thousands on the Mall safely. Afterward, Troy took Bill and Joe aside and said, "For some fun, I want to go to the D.C. Eagle tonight."

"Are you nuts? That's a notorious gay leather bar."

"Yeah, and it's Saturday night, and the place will be rock'n."

So, reluctantly, Bill and Joe accompanied him and his entourage to the D.C. Eagle where Troy found a gallant beau named Rick with which to have some fun.

"Troy, Rick has a leather bag that's making clanking sounds. We're going to have to check to see what's in his bag."

Troy looked at Bill and winked, "Don't worry about it. I know exactly what's in the bag."

Troy had fun that night in his hotel suite with Master Rick.

One of Troy' ardent admirers was a pastor at the National Cathedral, which, as cathedrals go, is a very big deal.

The pastor asked, "Troy, would you like a special tour of the National Cathedral? I have the key to the Canterbury Pulpit."

"Lord Jesus, I would love to see the cathedral and stand in the very same pulpit where Martin Luther King Jr. preached his last Sunday sermon just ten years ago."

When they walked into the cathedral people were silently praying, most with rosary beads. As they walked down the nave aisle, their footsteps echoed off the tall gothic walls. The pastor opened the stanchion and led the small entourage onto the alter. He then unlocked the chain protecting the Canterbury Pulpit with its elaborate panels and stone carvings, one of which features the Archbishop of Canterbury handing the Magna Carta to King John for his signature.

Troy proudly mounted the pulpit, looked out across the gigantic gothic cathedral, then down at his entourage and his security detail. In a booming voice, he called out to the far corners of the cathedral, "Ladies and gentlemen, we're here today to join these two wonderful men in holy matrimony!"

Schneid and Joe laughed as the praying worshippers dropped their
rosary beads onto the hard marble floor.

THROWN UNDER THE BUS

"The first thing we do, let's kill all the lawyers."
- William Shakespeare

"Global Projects. How may I be of assistance?"

"This is Horace Schwein, Associate General Counsel of eBay. We are looking to hire an investigative company to handle a fraud investigation assignment. We'll be coming down to Beverly Hills from the Bay Area next week and would like to know if we could interview you and your team."

"Yes, we would love to meet with you."

"You should know that we will also be interviewing several Fortune 500 investigative firms, such as Pinkertons, Kroll, and Burns.

Schneid thought, "We don't stand a snowball's chance in hell to get their business when up against the three biggest worldwide firms. However, he agreed to meet with them."

It wasn't a pleasurable interview, so when Schneid's team walked out, they were sure they would not get the business. As Schneid drove through West Hollywood a couple of days later, his secretary called him, "Dr. Schneid, eBay's General Counsel is on the phone and would like to speak with you."

"Fine, please transfer the call to my cell phone."

"This is Dr. Schneid. How may I be of assistance?"

"Dr. Schneid, this is Fran Furter, General Counsel of eBay. How are you doing today, Dr. Schneid?"

"Excellent Ms. Furter."

"Good. Dr. Schneid, I am pleased to award Global Projects the fraud investigation assignment we discussed with you. Also, we want your firm to handle all future eBay fraud cases, both domestic and international. If you accept, we'll fly you up here as soon as possible to brief you and have you sign an NDA, a nondisclosure agreement."

When Schneid heard the news, he nearly rear-ended the car in front of him.

As he sat back in his office chair, he thought to himself, "We need more manpower to handle the eBay account. We need computer experts. No, we need computer technicians who know their way around the web and who can pierce fraudulent website security walls."

He spoke with his associate, "Carl, find a half dozen of Los Angeles' top teenage hackers. Since they'll be underage, get their parents to sign releases to allow them to work for us. Whatever you do, don't let them touch our computers or let them get into our system."

They hired six fifteen-year-old hackers to be the cadre of Global Projects' frontline fraud defense program. After several months, eBay was impressed with the team's work.

"Dr. Schneid, my team would like to fly down sometime this month to meet your top-notch counter-fraud investigative team."

Schneid wasn't about to let them see their team of fifteen-year-olds working mostly out of their parents' homes.

"Frank, we do top-secret work here for the government. Unless you have high-level, top-secret clearance from the government, we can't have you come down to our office."

"Oh, uh, that we don't have. Sorry to have bothered you with the request."

"No problem whatsoever, Frank. If and when you ever receive the appropriate clearances, we'll be more than happy to oblige."

Schneid also hired several adult investigators to fly around the U.S. and to other countries to meet with various law enforcement agencies while pursuing organized fraud activities. It was a big operation that lasted four years. Global Projects put a lot of corrupt people in jail and cleaned up all kinds of illegal on-line eBay seller sites.

One day, he got a call from eBay. "Dr. Schneid, if you get a sub-poena from the Southern District of New York, notify us right away."

"Why would I get a subpoena from them?"

"Just notify us."

Schneid thought to himself, "Why won't they tell me why. I'm their investigative arm, and you would think they would want me to know. There's something not right with this. wouldn't put it past them to throw me under the bus if it involves Glo-bal."

To protect himself and Global, Schneid immediately con-tacted the Southern District's Assistant U.S. Attorney (AUSA) Weisen to find out why. When he learned that it was about fire-arms, he volunteered to assist them with their investigation. In essence, he became Weisen's "deep throat."

"Dr. Schneid, not to worry, I promise that all of your commu-nications with my office will be kept confidential, especially from eBay and its lawyers."

"If you do, I'll be sued for violating our NDA with them."

Schneid then hired an ex-ATF agent to go over ten thousand eBay firearms' transactions to determine whether any had vio-lated federal law. None had.

One day out of the blue, Schneid got a subpoena from Wei-sen's office for him to appear before a federal grand jury in-vestigating eBay's involvement in dealings of firearms. He told Schneid not to alert or speak with anyone at eBay or to its law-yers about the subpoena to maintain a "Chinese Wall" to prevent legal conflicts of interests between associates.

Schneid flew back to New York and gave secret testimony to the grand jury. He described some of eBay's internal processes, how his company performed for them, and that they had found no improper firearms' transactions on eBay.

A year after giving testimony to the grand jury, Schneid was subpoenaed again, this time to appear at a pre-trial hearing in New York. He did so with a high-end lawyer from Washington D.C. paid for by eBay.

The day turned out to be a personal disaster for him.

"Dr. Schnide, do you recall phoning me at the U.S. Attorney's office to offer assistance with our investigation of illegal sales of firearms on eBay's platform?"

Stunned, Schneid realized that she had just broken her confidentiality agreement with me." She put him in a terrible fix.

He knew he should say, "Yes, I did." However, I did, if he admitted that under oath, the eBay lawyers sitting in the courtroom would know that he had broken his NDA with them.

Humiliated and angry, he struck back with, "Mrs. Weisen, my name is Dr. Schneid, not Schnide. I do remember speaking with you, but to the best of my ability, I can't recall any of the specifics of what we discussed. It must be because of the pain medications I am currently taking."

"Dr. Schnide, do you recall testifying in front of the grand jury about specific security protocols of eBay before the grand jury?"

"AUSA Weisen, that's Dr. Schneid, and no, I do not recall testifying about any specifics."

"Dr. Schnide, you seem to be having trouble remembering anything about calling my office or about your testimony of a year ago before the grand jury."

"I can explain that."

"Oh, please do."

"Well, you see, every single time you address me, you refer to me as Dr. Schnide, and I have to keep correcting you to say, 'It's Dr. Schneid.' I assume you are not on the same mind-clouding medications as I am. Yet your consistent inability to remember how to pronounce my name correctly is only separated by brief moments in time. At the same time, you're asking me to recall details of a telephone conversation from almost a year and a half ago, along with details of testimony before the grand jury from a year ago."

The judge smirked, leaned over the bench and said, "Dr. Schneid, I find your testimony to be fairly incredible. However, Mrs. Weisen, I think the doctor has sufficiently answered your question."

On the way to the airport, Schneid called his associate, "Carl, it was a witch hunt, plain and simple. The matter won't go to trial, and both sides wasted millions of dollars. It's over. The notorious Southern District of New York was trying to make a name for itself again by going after a giant like eBay.

"Worst of all, to keep us from being sued for violating our NDA to help them, I perjured myself for the first time in my professional career. For me, it was an absolute nightmare. That bitch Weisen stuck a knife in my back and threw me under the bus by breaking every confidentiality promise she made to me."

SELLING MISSILES &
THE HELICOPTERS

Schneid's secretary walked into his office and said, "Bill, an official letter from the Air Force, just came in for you."
Schneid opened it and read:

The Department of the Air Force
Office of Special Investigations
Andrews Air Force Base, Maryland

Dear Dr. Bill Schneid:

Please accept this letter of appreciation for bringing to our attention the attempted sale of a Nike surface to air missile, the Black Hawk attack helicopter and the distribution and sale of other sensitive military equipment.

The outstanding support given by you and your organization enhanced the efforts of our investigators and allowed them to move forward on this most sensitive issue. This could have had multiple serious effects on our national security. Thanks to your interception, we and the Department of Defense were able to prevent several serious threats from being realized.

Again, thank you for your outstanding support in these matters.

Sincerely,

Francis X. Taylor
Brigadier General, USAF, Commander
Office of Special Investigations

Schneid noticed the letter was not dated, so he rang up the general's office and spoke with his secretary.

"Dr. Schneid, the general specifically asked me not to date the letter for reasons of national security. You do realize don't you that this and other incidents you have reported to us can never be made public?"

"I certainly do and please pass along my sincere thanks to the general. I realize that he doesn't write many of these letters."

"Dr. Schneid, I've been working with Brigadier General Thompson for almost four years, and he's never written a letter like this to anyone but you."

During Schneid's tenure with eBay as their chief investigator, he and his team regularly perused the platform to see if people were selling illegal items. Late one evening, Schneid came across an auction out of Florida for a Nike Hercules guided missile. The same seller was offering a Black Hawk Attack Helicopter in another auction.

"Well, these are obviously ridiculous. Nobody sells a guided missile or an attack helicopter. How would you even get these things? This can't be for real."

Using his eBay undercover name with a false profile and rating as cover, Schneid sent a message to the seller.

"I'm interested but only if the missile is functional and it comes with its ground system."

Ten minutes later, he got a response.

"It's fully functional. I used to work on these things. It includes a working ground system. The propulsion and guidance systems are intact, but obviously, it lacks the XW-7 nuclear warhead components."

It was now around midnight Pacific time when Schneid rang up the Air Force's Office of Special Investigations unit in Maryland. Some private at the command center sleepily answered his call.

"Private, I need to speak to somebody above your pay grade."

"They're all asleep."

Nobody low in the ranks wants to wake up higher ranking officers because they think their superiors will yell at them.

"I don't care if they are all asleep. I need somebody above you now."

Finally, he got some lieutenant on the line. "Listen, a guy is trying to sell a Nike Hercules missile and a Black Hawk attack helicopter."

"What?"

"That's right, and please take this seriously. Check it out on eBay. Here are the auction site numbers. Get access to the internet and take a look at it. Time is of the essence because the auction ends in less than four hours."

The lieutenant looked them up. "Holy shit, you're right."

"Of course, I'm right. I'm a retired Colonel and a criminal investigator. I know my shit. Now alert your commander and get on it before any bad guys buy this stuff."

After corresponding with him back and forth several times, the Air Force became convinced that this guy was for real and most likely possessed the military equipment. Once they determined his exact location, they got agents to his home where they found the missile and helicopter in a barn on his farm.

So how did this guy find the missile and helicopter? People with the know-how could buy parts of demilitarized equipment like helicopters and missiles and put them together. Sometimes there were whole sections or units available. You could even purchase enough parts and make a functional tank.

eBay also had a category for government surplus items. While looking through that section, Schneid found such an auction listing for part #46793-A. It had a starting bid of three thousand dollars and had active bidders.

Schneid thought, "What the fuck is that? What military part would cost so much and why are so many people interested?"

So, he got hold of a Department of Defense's Defense Criminal Investigative Service.

"Hello, this is Agent Mike Cranford. How may I be of assistance?"

Schneid explained what he had found.

"You need to establish some type of unit to start tracking this stuff down because this is way too weird. I've got a part number with no description and some ridiculous bidding going on. I have no idea what this part is. Do you?"

"Will you hold while I look up the part number?"

"Sure, I'll hold."

After a while, Cranford came back and said, "That's the decryption module to a frontline decryption radio."

"Really? Well, then I wonder who is doing the bidding. They would be people who know what that part is."

"We'll investigate right away."

"Since I am head of eBay's investigative unit, I might be of assistance."

They took him up on his offer and discovered that foreign

government agents had been using eBay as an arms' buying and distribution platform.

During his tenure with eBay, Schneid and his team continued to work with the Department of Defense to ensure the closure of all auctions that posed national security risks.

THE TURD IN THE CHIEF'S PUNCHBOWL

"Power corrupts; absolute power corrupts absolutely."
- Lord Action

Thanks to early Spanish influence, there are over thirty-three cities in California named after Catholic saints. Unfortunately, in terms of corruption, one of those "saintly" cities hasn't always lived up to its namesake.

Along with thousands of other small and medium-sized cities across the nation, San Bernardino can fire their police chief and other high command police officers "at-will." That means any commanding police officer served at the pleasure of the mayor or other top city officials and can be fired by them "without cause." If a chief or senior officer personally offends, uncovers city-government corruption or does something politically at odds with anybody above him or her, they could be fired immediately. The result is that corruption within these city governments is allowed to persist.

It happens more frequently than you think and is not in the public's best interest for a city to have in its charter. Many larger cities have come to realize this and have formed police commissions with civilian members to use due process to deal with police matters and officials.

Many police chiefs use smaller cities as step-ladders to land higher-paying chief jobs in larger cities or to qualify for higher-paying positions in the private security sector. Those near retirements don't want to rock any boats because they want their nice sweet retirement police pensions. So, very few at-will chiefs want to do anything that would jeopardize their careers or retirement bliss. In cities with at-will chiefs, a lot of problematic stuff gets swept under the rug. Such was the case with the "saintly" city called San Bernardino when its police chief asked Schneid to investigate possible internal corruption.

"Bill, I inherited a turd in my punchbowl, and I need it to go away."

"Ok, Chief Gilman, tell me about your turd?"

"Well, I have a couple of controversial internal investigation reports. One is called "On-Ice," and it's about holding people without cause, and the other is about corruption within our narcotics unit. Some here say that both reports are less than complete and amount to cover-ups. So it seems I've inherited a rat's nest of corruption in my department and maybe elsewhere in the city government."

"Wow, you've only been on the job for about a month, and you're already embroiled in this?"

"Yes, it seems that the former chief had a lot of unresolved issues. Bill, I need someone with your extensive expertise to look into these? I need someone I can trust to find out the truth. I need these problems to go away. Interested in helping me out?"

"Dr. Schneid, you don't know me, but I'm being indicted on a conspiracy to sell drugs. Word on the street tells me that you're a trustworthy and straight-shooting cop. I have a problem with some corrupt cops that I think you should know about."

"Jim, I can't promise you that I can make your problem go away, but I will look into it, and I won't name you as my source for anything you tell me in confidence. Capisce?"

"Capisce. That's what I needed to hear. Listen, my drug case hasn't gone to trial yet, so I don't want anybody knowing it was me who told you what I'm about to tell you.

"You have my word."

"When the narcotics unit executed their search warrant of my house, they wrote down that they seized fifty thousand dollars from my home safe. That's not right, because I had a hundred thousand dollars in it. I don't know where the other fifty thousand disappeared to."

"Got it. I'll look into it and let you know what I find out. Stay tuned."

Schneid called to let the chief know about the cash discrepancy.

"Oh my god. Are you shittin me! They kept $50,000 for themselves! What else have you got, Bill?"

"Oh, that's just the tip of the iceberg. Wait 'til you hear this. A few of your narcotics unit detectives have been handing out thousands of dollars to informants without having the transactions witnessed by one of their "brothers" or "sisters." The narcotics detectives not doing it know about it, but haven't reported it to Internal Affairs."

"What?"

"Yep, whenever they took a draw from the narcotics' Snitch-Fund they filled out their CID (Confidential Informant Disbursement) reports with their names and the actual names of their informants."

"My God, that's not only stupid but dangerous to everyone involved, especially our informants."

"Oh, and that's not all. They also have been giving fake case numbers to their snitch payments and not been including the informant-signed payment receipts. They're not writing down what the payments are specifically for and they've been leaving blank the witness-of-payment section.

"So, there's no way to know how much of that money they kept and how much of it they paid to their informants. I interrogated a half dozen of your narcotics detectives. You could see the sweat pouring off their brow as I drilled them. They knew I had them."

"So, do you think the previous chief knew about this?"

"Of course he did. He'd have to be a complete ignoramus to not know about the graft and corruption. I mean, all he had to do was read their reports. Look, chief, everybody in the narcotics' unit and up the chain is suspect, if not corrupt, including the former Chief of Police. Cover your ass and tread lightly."

"Thanks for the heads up and keep on digging. I'll need more than what you've given me to clean this shit-house."

"Chief, Bill here. Listen, I've been looking into your "On-Ice" report. One of the cases investigated involved a woman named Wilma. A police sergeant's house got burglarized, and prints on the front doorknob came back to a guy named Germaine who was on probation for a prior burglary. The detectives found out that Germaine lived with his mother. Without a warrant, they busted into her Fontana condo looking for him but only found a couple of children and their young mother, Wilma.

"Neither Wilma or her mother knew where Germaine was. Pissed off, racist, and probably misogynist, the detectives arrested his sister on a trumped-up parole violation charge, took her to jail and kept her "on-ice" until her brother turned himself in the next evening."

"How did they get the brother to come in?"

"The lead detective traced his cell phone and found him in Las Vegas. The detective told him they would hold his sister in jail unless he turned himself in and also threatened to send her children to child protection services."

Wilma hadn't committed any crimes, but they interrogated her and put her "on-ice" in jail for a day. Wilma's mother filed a civil rights complaint with the DA's office, but no investigators were ever assigned to interview her. When Schneid learned of this, he did what the DA's office should have already done. He questioned her.

"Dr. Schneid, my Wilma was deeply wronged by them officers, but I

don't want no attorney. I just want the San Bernardino District of Attorney to investigate this to make sure this never happens again, not to her, not to no one."

Schneid left his card with her and said, "Mam, if you ever need any legal advice or any related help, you call me."

"Why, blessed-be-the-Lord, you really believe me... don't you."

"Damn right, I believe you."

Wilma had been kidnapped, held hostage and extorted by the police detectives. Schneid also wanted to learn why the District of Attorney hadn't followed up with Wilma's mother. He contacted them to go over with them her case. Mysteriously, the DA's office refused to investigate her claim. They had already made some questionable plea deals with similar police misbehavior. So Schneid contacted a friend who was a chief executive within the office of the state's Attorney General.

"Look, Bill, I would love for us to prosecute this case, but we can't because protocol demands the Chief must first ask our San Diego office to investigate."

Schneid remembered that there was always at least one ATF agent embedded in the city's narcotics' task force. So, he brought his evidence to the ATF.

"Dr. Schneid, as the ATF attorney in charge of this region, I cannot allow you to interview any of our agents unless you can give me the proper authorization to do so."

Undeterred, Schneid contacted the closest FBI's Civil Rights Unit. He explained who he was and what he had learned during his internal affairs investigation.

"Was this woman, Wilma, hurt?"

"No, she wasn't hurt, but she was kidnapped and held for extortion by people who are supposed to protect her civil rights."

"Can you hold?"

A few minutes later, Agent Hunt returned. "Dr. Schneid, I don't think we're interested in your case."

"Why not? By doing what they did, they obviously violated her civil rights."

"We're just not interested."

"So, you're telling me that for somebody's civil rights to be abridged, they have to suffer physical injury? Since when has that become a defining element of whether or not the FBI will take on a civil rights' case?"

"Look, Dr. Schneid, I'm not going to argue with you. We're not going to take the case, and that's final."

"Well, agent Hunt, it's heartwarming to see the FBI so concerned about somebody's civil rights."

Since nobody in law enforcement on any level would investigate the case, Schneid turned to the press. He essentially became the deep throat to a couple of newspapers telling them what questions to ask. Articles about a possible police department conspiracy and cover-up involving the District of Attorney started appearing in the papers. The whole city was on edge.

Trouble for the city didn't stop there. Chief Gilman had only made a verbal agreement with Schneid to do an internal investigation and put no time or monetary limits on his work. When Schneid handed him a $60,000 bill, the chief almost had a heart attack. Neither of them had imagined how deep the corruption was and how much extra time it would take for Schneid to expose all of it.

The chief contacted Schneid, and they negotiated a much lower amount. However, the amount was still way over what the chief was legally entitled to contract for without the City Council's approval. So, Schneid sued and won his case before a non-binding arbiter. The City Attorney reviewed the finding and said, "Since it's non-binding arbitration, we're not going to give you another nickel." However, Schneid persisted, and they wound up settling for an additional amount.

Schneid's experiences with San Bernardino opened his eyes as to how corrupt small and medium-sized cities could be. He had never seen such a rotten police department. No wonder the city consistently ranked in the bottom ten of the worst U.S. cities in which to live. It was just one big mess.

The chief had inherited more than just a small turd. He had inherited what turned out to be a huge turd of politics, intrigue, and conspiracy that he thought was too hot to handle. He retired a year later, and nobody lost their jobs because nobody ever followed through to correct the corruption exposed by Schneid.

SMILEY-FACED OSAMA BIN LADEN

"Bill, when it comes to secretive government missions, the public usually only knows what the government wants the public to know via press releases and interviews. What happened to Osama bin Laden is a bit different from what the government told the public."

Schneid and his two ex-special forces friends looked out over the zoo's oasis exhibit as they told their version of how the U.S. actually took care of Osama Bin Laden.

"Bill, I was part of the ground team that surveilled his compound and Dirk was on board the Carl Vinson to identify and dispose of bin Laden at sea."

"Rick and I saw what Obama and his security team at the White House team saw from the SEAL's helmet cams, but only eight of us were on the Vinson to witness the sea burial."

"How is it that the Pakistanis didn't alert us as to his whereabouts? Elements in their government must have known."

"Maybe so, but to this day, we're not sure which, if any, of our Pakistani counterparts, knew where he was hiding."

"You mean to tell me that no Pakistani military or government officials noticed this huge compound surrounded by barbed wire and everything and wondered who lives there. Osama's compound was just a short distance from a military academy and installations. "

"As I said, we don't know if they knew. We do know that they were super pissed off at us after the operation."

"Rick, why didn't they take him alive? I mean, with the element of complete surprise combined with SEAL firepower and wherewithal, why wasn't he taken out alive? After all, we're supposedly a country of laws, and we could have brought him to justice by trying and convicting him, similar to what we did to Noriega."

"Yeah, the order was to take him alive, if possible, but we knew the SEALS were going to kill him, if possible, period. There was too much hatred in their minds after 9/11, so there's no way they would have taken him alive. Also, can you imagine the backlash from the Muslim countries if we had held him for trial? It would have brought on an onslaught of attacks across the world. "

"Understood. We saw Obama go down and it's fair to say that he was summarily executed."

"The SEALs helicoptered the body back to our base in Jalalabad, Afghanistan and then to the carrier USS Carl Vinson where Dirk's unit took his DNA to make sure he was who we thought he was."

"Yeah, we got a positive match and then decided how to deal with the body's disposal. We didn't bring him to any country for a land burial because that would have given Al Qaeda a martyr's monument site to rally around. Anyhow, Dirk was on board the Vinson and can tell you how they handled the body."

"The official Pentagon press reports claimed that his body was washed and wrapped in a white cotton shroud and buried at sea within twenty-four hours per religious instructions. They got those parts right, but they also claimed that an imam was on board to do all that and to give the Islamic last rites. The problem is, we didn't have an imam aboard the ship or in our battle group, so we took one of our team members who spoke fluent Arabic, put a baseball hat on his head backward and gave him a Koran to read. After he read the rites, we put the Koran with the body because we didn't want anybody to get hold of it and use it as a religious relic."

"I imagine there were a lot of sailors who wanted to do some damage to the body."

"You bet, but we kept it out of sight from the crew in a secure area to do what needed to be done."

"Dirk, tell him the sick humorous part."

"Well, we found a roll of three-inch diameter smiley-face stickers and secured the edges of the large cotton body shroud with them."

"You didn't!"

"We did, and we put one on his forehead before we tied weights onto the body, but not too heavy as to take it to the bottom where the sharks wouldn't touch it. We wanted it to float just below the surface in the shark zone where it would get picked clean and disappear. In the middle of the night, we moved the body over to an elevator on the hangar deck and laid it on top of a platform, tilted and slid Mr. bin Laden into Davy Jones' locker."

Have a nice day!

*[**Not** For Immediate Release: 5/3/11]*

"Early in the morning of May 3, 2011, Osama bin Laden's body was dropped into the deepest waters of the North Arabian Sea with a yellow smiley-face on his forehead."

CREAMING TRICARE FOR
EASY MONEY

"If your attack is going too well, you have
walked into an ambush."
- U.S. Infantry Journal

"So, the Tricare medical scam is now looking to be billions of dollars! Holy shit, this thing has gone from tens of thousands to billions. Dr. Schneid, I've been sitting on this for over a year. It's huge. May I publish what I have in *The Tennessean*."

"No, Brett, it's not over. I've fed you information on the premise that you will not publish it until I tell you it's time. The government hasn't finished their investigations, and their initial indictments are still sealed. Wait for a court unsealing. Don't worry. You'll have a big head start on every journalist in the country. In the meantime, I'll continue to be your 'Deep Throat' on this."

"Alright, I'll hold off and wait for your go-ahead. I'm sweating because CBS News just did a segment about it."

"Yeah, I saw it, but their story was not about the marines. You still have the exclusive on that."

Retired Lt. Colonel Schneid drove to Marine Corps Air Ground Combat Center Twentynine Palms, the most extensive Marine base in the U.S., to investigate a marine accused of prostituting himself. Maybe hundreds of marines were involved, more than all of the branches combined. Since junior enlisted marine pay is so meager, they were looking for extra spending money.

The marine he was to interview was answering and placing ads on Craigslist to prostitute himself for between two hundred fifty and five hundred dollars a session.

At one point, Schneid asked him, "What else do you do for money?"

"Well, Sir, I get paid to fill out doctor forms for a couple of kinds of prescription cream: one for pain and the other for scars."

"Private, do you have a copy of that doctor's form?"

The marine showed Schneid his fill-in-the-blanks order form.

"Sir, I fill out this form and send it via fax, scan/email, or mail it to this doctor's office in Tennessee. I get a phone call from some assistant at the doc's office, and they write me a prescription. Then I get the two creams once a month from some pharmacy, and Tricare covers the cost."

"That's it? You don't speak with any doctor or physician's assistant?

"That's correct, Sir, I don't."

"Ok, so you fill out this form, and you get paid how much?"

"Three hundred dollars a pop for each prescription."

"How often?"

"Once every six months."

"How do you get paid."

"Direct deposit into my savings account."

"Do these creams help?"

"I don't know. I just got this stuff."

"What pharmacy do they come from?"

"A pharmacy in Utah."

"What does this stuff look like?"

The private showed Bill his two plastic blue tubes.

He studied their compounded ingredients. Schneid had done medical audits before and immediately realized these were not creams for pain or scars. They were virtually the same ingredients used in cheap over-the-counter face creams and moisturizers.

"Private, if you don't mind, I'd like to keep these?"

"Yes, Sir, you can keep both."

"How did you find out about getting this stuff?"

"From my roommate, Private Josh Morgan."

"How did your roommate find out about it?"

"I don't know, Sir. He never told me. All I know is he gets a kickback every time I send in an order. He said I could make more if I recruited others to do the same thing."

Schneid drove back to his office and decided to send a message to the Tricare hotline. He knew a health care fraud when he saw one and this one he suspected might reach far and wide. Plus, he had the evidence in hand.

The Tricare representative responded, "How may I be of service?"

With two fingers, he typed his reply explaining that he had uncovered a fraudulent multi-level marketing scheme.

"Sir, this sounds like some sort of phishing scam to steal your private information. Make sure you don't give any of your personal information over the phone. Thank you very much, and have a nice day."

An hour later he sent another message, this time listing his credentials as a criminologist and private investigator, what he had uncovered in more detail and finally that he was in possession of evidence to prove his case.

"This is a significant health care fraud. You need to get on it."

"Thank you, Sir, for all of your information. We will get back to you."

Three days later, Schneid got a call from an investigator from the Department of Defense's Office of the Inspector General asking if she could fly out to California to meet with him and inspect his evidence. She did, along with two NCIS investigators from Twentynine Palms.

As a Private Investigator, what Schneid uncovered was just the tip of the iceberg. It became America's largest and most far-reaching health care fraud in history. Tricare had been billed $14,500 for each of the thousands of tubes of cream. Estimates of how much the six hundred plus person network defrauded Tricare was estimated to be between twelve and fifteen billion dollars, and yes, Brett eventually got the scoop on the marines' involvement and published it in *The Tennessean*.

$14,500 tube of cream

APPENDIX - SCHNEID'S AWARDS & ACCOLADES

THE
FEDERAL BUREAU OF INVESTIGATION

EXPRESSES ITS APPRECIATION TO

Dr. William H. Schneid
Global Projects, Ltd.

FOR
EXCEPTIONAL SERVICE IN THE PUBLIC INTEREST

May 2003

DATE

DIRECTOR

- Robert S. Mueller III, signatory -

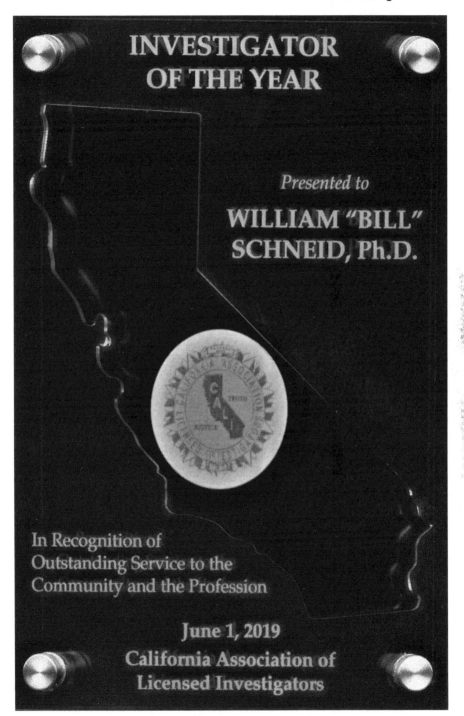

DEPARTMENT OF THE AIR FORCE
AIR FORCE OFFICE OF SPECIAL INVESTIGATIONS
ANDREWS AIR FORCE BASE MD

AFOSI/CC
1535 COMMAND DR AVE, SUITE 302
ANDREWS AFB MD 20762

Mr. William Schneid
Global Projects
520 Washington Blvd Suite 500
Marina del Rey, CA 90292

Dear Mr. Schneid

Please accept this letter of appreciation for bringing to our attention the attempted sale of a Nike Surface-to-Air Missile. The outstanding support given by you and your organization enhanced the efforts of our investigators and allowed them to move forward on this most sensitive issue. This could have had a serious affect on our national security.

Thanks to your interception, we were able to prevent a serious threat from being realized. It's reassuring to know that there are citizens like yourself who share our concern for public safety. Again, thank you for your outstanding support in this matter.

Sincerely

FRANCIS X. TAYLOR
Brigadier General, USAF
Commander

"PRESERVING OUR LEGACY, PROTECTING THE FUTURE."

Operation Lion's Den Joint Federal Narcotics Task Force
Presents, With Honor, To
WILLIAM H. SCHNEID
THE MEDAL OF HONOR
For displaying extraordinary, gallantry, bravery, and heroism
by saving the lives of innocent civilians and comrades while
under heavy weapons fire and while being in a hostile foreign country.
Further, after being captured by hostile drug cartel members,
he created and executed an escape plan resulting in the freeing
of fellow comrades. In so doing, and with total disregard for his
personal safety, he incurred several bullet wounds. Undaunted,
he continued his mission and alone captured four significant
fugitives from justice.
September 10, 1970

CERTIFICATE
OF
APPRECIATION

Bureau of Alcohol, Tobacco, Firearms and Explosives

Presented to

William H. Schneid, Ph.D.

Criminologist/Director of Special Operations
Apex Strategic Investigations Group La Quinta

In appreciation for your assistance to the
Bureau of Alcohol, Tobacco, Firearms and Explosives, Los Angeles Field Division.

Special Agent in Charge
Los Angeles Field Division

January 07, 2011
Date

Federal Emergency Management Agency
Region IV Administration and Resources Planning Division
Information Technology Services Branch

Certificate of Appreciation

Presented to:

Bill Schneid, Ph. D.

GLOBAL PROJECTS, LTD
Investigative Research Analyst
"tempus omnia revelat"

In recognition of Outstanding Cyber Investigations,
dedication and exemplary service to the Agency
and the United States of America.

November 17, 2002

Jeffrey Shiff
Information Technology Services
Branch Chief

W. Greg Burel
Administration and Resources Division
Division Director

DEPARTMENT OF DEFENSE
MISSILE DEFENSE AGENCY
7100 DEFENSE PENTAGON
WASHINGTON, DC 20301-7100

21 September 2006

Apex Strategic Investigations Group
578 Washington Blvd.
Suite 500
Marina Del Rey, CA 90292

Attention: William H. Schneid Ph.D.

Dear Dr. Schneid,

I am writing to thank you for providing me with some of the most up-to-date information and best analyzed reports on international events available in the world today. As an intelligence collector and analyst for twenty years, I can say with confidence that your material outshines most of what's out there.

SleuthOne not only gives a quick look at the latest global events, including breaking-news stories, but it puts these events in context through lucid think pieces that are often provocative and always informative. I am continually amazed at how quickly you and your team are able to synthesize complex data on just about any national security topic. It seems that within minutes of an event you have ready-to-go, hard-hitting analysis that beats everyone else.

In a world clogged with information, your reports are refreshing and exceptional. Quite frankly, doing without my morning dose of SleuthOne would be like denying a coffee addict his triple java. I have to have it.

Sincerely,

Chief, Analysis and Scenarios
Directorate for Intelligence
Missile Defense Agency

Presented to

DR. WILLIAM H. SCHNEID, Ph.D.

In recognition and appreciation of your
outstanding contributions and support
of the
Intelligence mission of the
Bureau of Alcohol, Tobacco,
Firearms and Explosives,
Office of Strategic
Intelligence and Information, and for your
distinguished leadership, professionalism
and dedication to a grateful nation.

Washington, D.C.

Presented to

WILLIAM H. SCHNEID, Ph.D.

Criminologist-Director of Special Operations
Apex Strategic Investigations Group

In recognition of your
dedicated service and
outstanding relationship with ATF
You are a consummate, prompt professional
who has extended himself to the
ATF Family and we are fortunate
to have such an invaluable
and credible resource.

From your friends at ATF
June 2010

DEPARTMENT OF DEFENSE
BALLISTIC MISSILE DEFENSE ORGANIZATION
7100 DEFENSE PENTAGON
WASHINGTON, DC 20301-7100

May 23, 2000

Global Projects Ltd.
520 Washington Blvd.
Suite 500
Marina Del Rey, CA 90292

Attn: Bill Schneid
      Director, Special Operations

Dear Mr. Schneid:

    I am writing to compliment your analysts for their
consistently well-written, objective, and insightful
reports on international current events. The pieces are
just the right length and evince a remarkable clarity that
is very hard to find anywhere else, inside or outside the
government. As a former analyst and speech writer myself,
I have a special appreciation for high-quality
communication skills and keen understanding of complex
issues.

    Your folks are among the best I have seen, and I look
forward to reading many more of their reports. Thank you
for including me (and now one of my colleagues) on your
distribution list. Keep up the fine work.

              Sincerely,

              Assistant Director for
              Security, Counterintelligence, and
              Information Assurance

WILLIAM H. SCHNEID

DIRECTOR, SPECIAL OPERATIONS

GLOBAL PROJECTS, LTD.

IN RECOGNITION OF YOUR SUPPORT TO ATF

SAN FRANCISCO FIELD DIVISION

Presented to

WIILIAM SCHNEID

In recognition and appreciation of your
outstanding contributions to a
grateful nation and your distinguished
professionalism and dedication in promoting
the highest standards of law enforcement;
but mostly for your trust and friendship

Best wishes and Godspeed
from your friends and colleagues.

2019
Miami, Florida

The Los Angeles County Sheriff's Department

COMMENDATION

Dr. William H. Schneid, Ph.d

During the spring of 2009, you were contacted for technical assistance to locate two known 290 P.C registrants and sexual predators. Both Megan's Law registrants had failed to register with local law enforcement and were suspected of violating their conditions of parole as well as being involved in criminal activity. You assisted the Los Angeles County Sheriff's Department by unselfishly dedicating your resources, skills, and expertise to provide critical information leading to a successful investigation and protecting the residents of Los Angeles County.

July 24, 2009

*"I knew,
really knew
I would never die
with my song unsung."*

- Gary Russo

ABOUT THE AUTHOR

Gene Warneke is a lifelong and trusted friend of Bill Schneid. Gene is a former magazine and book editor and contributor, ghostwriter, photojournalist, English and social sciences instructor, and commercial and travel photographer. He has degrees in Anthropology and Social Science.

Gene has lived abroad for almost a third of his life in England, Australia, Mexico, and Costa Rica. He now lives near Palm Springs, California with his lovely wife, Maria.

You can reach Gene at authorgenew@gmail.com.

Made in the
USA
Columbia, SC

77979112R00107